Your eyes fourteen
The mad Greek dictionary

Your eyes fourteen

The mad Greek dictionary

By John Carr and Paul Anastasi

ATHENS NEWS

Copyright © John Carr and Paul Anastasi, 2007

All rights reserved

No part of this publication may be reproduced, stored in a retrieval system or transmitted, in any form or by any means, electronic, mechanical, photocopying, recording, or otherwise, without the prior written permission of the publisher, except brief quotes used in connection with reviews written specifically for inclusion in a magazine or a newspaper.

Proofreader: Dorde Crncevic
Designer: Yannis Smyrnis
Cover design: Stellios Livanos, Multimedia S.A.

Series editor: John Psaropoulos

ISBN 978-960-89200-3-3

Printed and bound in Athens, Greece by Psyllidis Graphic Arts
Pre-press by Multimedia SA

Contents

Foreword by John Carr IX

Anti-foreword by Paul Anastasi...XI

People and human relations 13

Body parts and sex 26

Animals, plants and food 39

Weather and nature 55

Life experiences 60

Historical memories 76

The otherworld 79

Foreword by John Carr

This book is a glance into the colourful world of Modern Greek idiolects.

An idiolect is a form of linguistic communication indigenous to any given nation, a form which shortcuts the more formal uses of grammar and syntax and employs vivid figurative language to illustrate its point.

Idiolects can come in the form of proverbs, expressions and argot. A proverb is a complete phrase illustrating an abstract point through a concrete example, with a self-contained structure and universally accepted metaphorical meaning, as in "an apple a day keeps the doctor away".

An expression is something shorter and often pithier and more inventive. It's usually not a grammatically complete main clause; more often it's a verbal or adverbial phrase of not more than half a dozen words that livens up the use of language but at the same time runs the ever-present danger of deteriorating into a cliche. (Unlike English, Greek still encourages the use of cliches, both written and spoken.) Sometimes an idiolectic expression becomes part of a certain stratified argot, sometimes not.

Greek is especially rich in idiolectic expressions. From Homer onwards, the imaginative use of words has been encouraged. The proverbial quick-wittedness of the Greeks has also played its part, bringing out the startling metonymic and synecdocheal possibilities lying concealed in even the most mundane concepts.

This is not a book of Modern Greek proverbs, though a few will be seen popping up among the idiolects listed and analysed here. The expressions are divided into seven broad categories according to their main subject: people and human relations; body parts and sex; animals, plants and food; weather and nature; life experiences; historical memories; and the otherworld. Some of these categories, to be sure, do overlap, and we hope the reader will forgive an occasional apparent inconsistency.

The majority of expressions will be seen to have emerged from the first four categories, suggesting their origin in the observation of human and natural phenomena common in the kind of pastoral and agricultural society which Greece was when the modern linguistic usage was being shaped in the 18th and 19th centuries.

Some of these expressions may seem crude to the genteel eye and ear, even *verboten* in a politically correct sense. But the Greeks have never been, and never will be, Puritan Protestants. In their vernacular the risque and the divine often intermingle, sometimes with startling results. For obvious reasons I have shunned the more obscene or blasphemous expressions. But long and hard thought was required over many entries. In the end I decided to include them on the assumption that most readers have more or less mature and open minds. But enough of a flavour of Greek usage, I think, has been given so that the reader can either enrich his or her knowledge of the language, or just sit back for an edifying read.

A note on the entry style: for the sake of grammatical uniformity the main English entries are phrased as gerunds, while the corresponding Greek employs the first-person conjugation (the so-called Greek infinitive). Whatever inconsistencies remain are purely my own.

Finally, a debt of gratitude is due to Theodora Kappou, who checked the text and corrected a few glaring errors through her constructive criticism. Thanks also to John Psaropoulos, editor of the *Athens News*, for enabling this work to see the light of day.

Athens, June 2006

Anti-foreword by Paul Anastasi

After many years abroad, Giorgos' younger brother Nikos wants to settle in Athens and do business in Greece. Giorgos believes that Nikos is naive about the ease with which he could live and work in Greece. It wouldn't exactly be like Odysseus returning home.

"Do you take me for a little American?" Nikos retorted. "I'm not going with cross in hand. I'll change their lights. The mountains are used to the snows."

"You'll all tangle your thighs," Giorgos said. "You'll make it a sea. They'll get the olive oil out of you. You've had it painted if you do business in Greece."

"As far as America is concerned I've cast a black stone behind me," Nikos said.

"They'll make your life a bicycle!" Giorgos cried. "They'll put your two feet into one shoe. They'll promise you hares with surplices but those will be words of the arse. You'll end up paying the hairs of your head. The result will be a hole in the water. You won't see a white day."

Nikos smiled. "Careful the chandelier! I don't eat stupid grass. I'll play it on two stages. At the bottom-bottom of the writing if I don't like it I'll become smoke."

"Live, May, to eat clover," Giorgos scoffed. "As much as you wash the black man, you'll only waste your soap. Don't write my advice on your old shoes."

A few days later Nikos relates his difficulties trying to set up a business.

"First I had to travel to the devil's mother. But I had luck a mountain and arrived with my soul in my mouth. So we spoke of winds and waters, and they told me curly hairs. I became bald. To call figs figs and a basin a basin, you were right. It doesn't burn them a nail to do business. They just want to make fast money."

"That's light lantern," Giorgos said. "You can beat on the deaf man's door as long as you like, it won't change things."

"Their ear doesn't sweat. But I'll still try. Bean, bean the bag fills."

"God the assistant," Giorgos said. "And remember, whatever you do, *your eyes fourteen!*"

What follows will help you decipher the above.

People and human relations

Biting the sheet metal - Δαγκώνω τη λαμαρίνα (Dangono ti lamarina)
. Meaning: falling in love
In a society where the excesses of romantic love have traditionally been regarded with a jaundiced eye, the image is apposite. Being totally besotted with someone is equated to being mentally ill. Sheet metal is perhaps the only material that would stand up to a frenzied gnashing of teeth. The phrase, by the way, is used almost entirely for men as, presumably, they are more prone to losing their wits in a romantic situation than women.

Blind man's justice - Του στραβού το δίκιο (Tou stravou to dikio)
Meaning: the other side of the argument; the benefit of the doubt
The term *stravos* means, besides a blind or partly-blind man, crooked or bent. The two meanings were once conflated, as blindness, like any physical infirmity, was in a harsh Balkan society seen as a defect with moral implications. Therefore to see the "other" side of an issue (something for which the Greek character is not famed) means to admit that "defective" people also can have a point.

Breaking them - Τα σπάμε (Ta spame)
Meaning: quarrelling, rupturing relations
As in many Greek expressions, the terms "it" and "them" are recruited to stand for a huge variety of life experiences and human situations. In this case, the image is that of snapping a physical bond such as a rope or chain. It can refer to either a personal or business breakup.

Chanting them - Τα ψέλνω (Ta pselno)
Meaning: telling off
As in much Greek slang, the "them" here refers not to the object of the action but the content of the action. In this case it's the collection of sharp words used in the process of berating someone.

The shrill tones might be reminiscent of the stentorian style of many Byzantine rite cantors, hence the reference to chanting.

Cleaning one - Καθαρίζω (Katharizo)
Meaning: murdering, putting out of the way
Deriving from the underworld, this expression is a cynical take on what happens when someone is murdered – "cleansed", that is, from the surface of the earth and from earthly associations.

An alternative meaning of **cleaning** is discharging one's debts or other obligations. The term carries a satisfying "clean" sense of one's honour kept intact.

Coming to the hands - Έρχομαι στα χέρια (Erhomai sta heria)
Meaning: getting into a fist fight
An argument can go through several stages: first angry words, then threatening gestures and, finally, physical grappling. If this is what the issue "comes" to, the hands (or fists) have their say.

Dropping it in front of one - Μου την πέφτει (Mou tin peftei)
Meaning: revealing one's true intentions; making a pass
The Greek syntax in this phrase is particularly tight, yet complex, indicating its probable birth in the working-class districts of Athens, not known for correct grammar. The image is that of a suitor finally "dropping" a mask (or perhaps dropping down to a kneeling position) and revealing his or her true feelings. The phrase is most often used in a romantic or relationship context.

It also carries a humiliating connotation for the dropper of the mask, as in **dropping one's face** (μου πέφτει η μούρη) *(mou peftei i mouri)*, meaning to lose face.

Every shirker to his bench - Κάθε κατεργάρης στον πάγκο του) (Kathe katergaris ston pango tou)
Meaning: duty calls; the day of reckoning is at hand
The expression could have emerged in the early industrial era, when most factory workers sat on benches. The Greeks have never internalised the puritan work ethic, thus the benches

could be empty for inexcusably long periods of time. The time to return to work, then, is the time to pay for the periods of shirking. Some attribute the origin of the phrase to prisons, where convicts had to line up seated on benches during the morning roll-call.

Finding them - Τα βρίσκουμε (Ta vriskoume)

Meaning: working things out; reaching a compromise

This very useful street phrase has warded off many a bitter quarrel. The "them" denotes the terms of agreement to be reached. For example, in a shop where bargaining takes place between buyer and seller, even though agreement is still far off, both will vow that "we'll find them" and remain on civil terms, confident that a solution will be found. It's a verbal signal that a fight would be in no one's interest. But, *caveat emptor,* the phrase can often be used to deceive, or lull one side into compliance.

Getting it turned - Μου στρίβει (Mou strivei)

Meaning: going mad; being driven insane

The origin of this image is obscure. It at first suggests someone's head becoming twisted, probably in motions suggesting madness.

The verb *strivo* (to turn or twist) is also often employed in its imperative form **turn!** (στρίβε!) *(strive!)* meaning get out of here, or about-face.

Good wreaths - Καλά στέφανα (Kala stefana)

Meaning: have a happy wedding

This is one of those strictly ritual phrases that the Greeks use at times of life-change such as baptisms, weddings and funerals. This particular one is brought into play when taking leave of an engaged couple (or either of the partners) who have presumably set a wedding date, and perhaps need to be encouraged - or warned - to stay on course. In this it's similar to **and to yours** *(qv)*, which, however, is reserved for those who are not yet engaged. In both cases the social pressure is subtle but highly effective.

Having it saved for someone - Του την έχω φυλαγμένη (Tou tin eho fylagmeni)
Meaning: plotting revenge
Part of the sweetness of revenge is the feeling of saving it up for an appropriate time. The grammatical structure is of interest, as it avoids the active voice and employs a participle that lends a vague air of additional menace.

Having them 400 - Τα 'χω τετρακόσια (Ta'ho tetrakosia)
Meaning: being alert and intelligent
The Greeks' use of the concept "many" tends to be expressed in multiplies of ten and four (see **Forty waves**, p 57). The figure most likely derives from the forty days which the Orthodox Church decrees for fasting and mourning. Four hundred is forty multiplied by ten, thus a greater emphasis on quantity or degree. A very clever person, then, could be conceptualized as "having four hundred" thoughts at once.

If my grandma had balls she'd be granddad - Αν η γιαγιά μου είχε αρχίδια, θα ήταν παπούλης (An i yaya mou eihe arhidia, tha itan papoulis)
Meaning: regrets about the past are futile
A pithy and colourful expression originating in northern Greece, whose inhabitants are known for their no-nonsense approach to life. It's an effective riposte to the what-if game.

It gives it to me - Μου τη δίνει (Mou ti dinei)
Meaning: it bothers me
The present indicative first-person is set out here as by far the most common grammatical form this phrase assumes. Essentially, it's a self-centred reaction.
On a deeper level the expression follows a tradition going back to Homer by apostrophising an abstract entity. The first "it" in the English translation refers to the thing that is bothersome. The second "it" is semantically more elusive; it's the sense of injustice which the bother generates in the victim.

The notion could be related to the so-called evil eye, a presumed spell hurled from one person onto another, that continues to terrify almost all Greeks.

On the other hand, it may simply be a case of the loose and imprecise vocabulary developed by semi-literate youths in the late 20th century cafe society.

It's got world - Έχει κόσμο (Ehei kosmo)

Meaning: there are a lot of people; it's crowded

Modern Greek has the unfortunate tendency to employ the same word for more than one meaning. An example is *kosmos,* which originally meant the adornment of Creation and subsequently came to mean the world in general. It also means people and public. But there is significance even here, because the average Greek never likes to be kept waiting; even a few people in a queue may seem like "the world".

Lame Mary - Κουτσή Μαρία (Koutsi Maria)

Meaning: just about everybody

This tight phrase encapsulates two old Greek negative stereotypes: women and the disabled.

Mary (or Maria) is one of the commoner Greek women's names, especially in the countryside where the Virgin Mary is more revered. Just after the Second World War, thousands of poor young village girls named Maria flocked to the cities seeking work. Many became housemaids in such numbers as to create a social stereotype noticeable even in Greek films of the period. A Maria who was also lame, though, would be at a rare disadvantage; not only would she be incapable of housework but also unlikely to find a husband, hence her position near the bottom of the social ladder.

The phrase has tended to come and go in waves, notably at times of rapid technological progress. Most recently, when mobile telephones became available to all, it was said that even lame Mary had one. One can also tell when a particular clothing fashion is about to become passe when smart ladies sniff that even lame Mary is wearing it nowadays.

Laughing - Γελάω (Yelao)

Meaning: cheating or deceiving

Greece's old negative social stereotypes include the naive or trusting person. Therefore, a successful deception or trick practised on someone would be the occasion for the perpetrator to laugh in evil glee. The usage these days carries only a mildly unfavourable connotation, and hence could be indicative of an ill-developed social conscience.

It's most often employed in the past tense, as in **they laughed you** (Σε γελάσανε) *(Se yelasane)* in the sense of "they've deceived you," or "you're kidding yourself."

Leaving in the cold of the bath - Αφήνω στα κρύα του λουτρού (Afino sta krya tou loutrou)

Meaning: leaving in the lurch

Except for the well-to-do, most Greeks didn't know what a hot bath was until well into the 20th century. Much personal cleanliness, as in ancient Sparta, had to make use of cold water. This is not generally a pleasant experience, and the shivering involved can be compared to the feeling of being abandoned.

The usage may also have a root in the ancient public baths ritual, in which a hot bath was followed by a cold one. If at any time the hot water was used up, then the bathgoer would have every reason to feel aggrieved.

Making a table - Κάνω τραπέζι (Kano trapezi)

Meaning: inviting one to dinner at home

The concepts of food and table have been conflated in the Greek tongue to the point at which the latter has become a metaphor for the former. What else was a table used for, if not to eat on?

Oriental influence is apparent here. Like many Middle Eastern peoples and the French, the Greeks value the way in which food is presented as much, or more than, the food *per se*. This seems to be because notions of personal honour dominate the proceedings, especially in the presence of guests. Much of the worth of the repast thus depends on what a laden table looks like rather than what it contains. Semantically, then, "table" thus becomes more important than "food".

Manolios undressed and put on his clothes another way
- Γδύθηκε ο Μανωλιός κι έβαλε τα ρούχα του αλλιώς (Gdythike o Manolios kai evale ta rouha tou allios)

Meaning: a change in name only; *plus ca change, plus c'est la meme chose*

Manolios is the Cretan colloquial form of the proper name Emmanuel (or Manolis in the rest of Greece). Thus we have a probable Cretan origin. On the other hand, the phrase in Greek carries a neat rhyme, which indicates that the form Manolios could have been picked for rhyming purposes.

What is certain is that the expression, like so many others, came from the old peasantry who had a salutarily sharp eye for hypocrisy and cant of any sort.

Mounting the cane - Καβαλάω το καλάμι (Kavalao to kalami)

Meaning: abusing authority; getting on a high horse

A metaphor for the principle that power corrupts.

In past eras young country boys everywhere would pretend to ride a horse by straddling a broomstick or cane. The image has stuck as denoting an immature handling of the reins by someone vain and despotic who becomes a petty tyrant by virtue of position.

Of the cuckold - Του κερατά (Tou kerata)

Meaning: blatant wrongdoing; the last straw

The Greek word for cuckold, *keratas,* means literally "the horned one". In Greece's heavily macho society, a cuckold is only one step above a homosexual, hence the common variation **of the homosexual** (του πούστη) *(tou pousti).* In the traditional view, the faults of cuckolds and homosexuals are too obvious to be tolerated.

Of the madwoman - Της τρελλής (Tis trellis)

Meaning: chaos, uproar

This is a socially polite version of **of the whore** *(qv).* Yet both are effective in portraying a sense of disorder or discredit, and equally commonly used. A screeching madwoman would not be the quietest or most circumspect of human beings, hence her house (indicated by the genitive "of") would be prone to a certain chaos.

One's violin - Το Βιολί μου (To violi mou)

Meaning: a stubbornly-held view, a monomania

In traditional Greek folk music, the violin usually has pride of place (alongside the clarinet) of furnishing the basic melody line. The violinist thus is tempted to go off on a tangent, fiddling away as the merriment rises, impervious to the other musicians. "Him and his violin" is a common wry reference to someone unheeding of arguments.

On the deaf man's door knock all you want - Στου κουφού την πόρτα όσο θέλεις βρόντα (Stou koufou tin porta oso theleis vronda)

Meaning: don't waste time with those who don't want to hear

The phrase in Greek, like so many others, carries a mild rhythmic cadence, placing it in the realm of proverbs rather than idiolects. It's included here for its conciseness and realism.

Yet, as with so many shrewd observations of human nature, it would appear to be at variance with the typical Greek character, which is not noted for its realism, either political or social. It must not be forgotten that most of these expressions originated in rural areas where the people, even today, employ fewer words and more common sense than the city types do.

Playing it - Το παίζω (To paizo)

Meaning: being insincere or phoney; playing a social role

A highly interesting phrase from the psychological aspect. The Greeks, as highly-skilled social actors, have always been astute at seeing through others' pretensions. The "playing" element refers mainly to intellectual and social pretenders acting above or below their station.

All modern Greek life is to some extent one vast theatre, where role-playing often is valued more than plain honesty and openness, traits that are too often seen as signs of naivete (see **With cross in hand,** p 83). Thus the mama who screams and threatens to kill herself at her son's choice of mate is playing as precisely defined a cultural role as anything seen on a stage.

Playing it two doors - Το παίζω δίπορτο (To paizo diporto)

Meaning: keeping one's options open; playing both sides of the field

Thanks partly to their peril-filled history, the Greeks even today prefer to avoid taking definite stands on whatever has an uncertain outcome. There's always the risk of ending up on the wrong or losing side. Thus, it's better to have a second "door" available if the first one slams shut.

Putting the glasses on one - Του βάζω τα γυαλιά (Tou vazo ta yalia)

Meaning: showing up one as inept; beating someone at his own game

Traditionally in Greece, glasses were worn only by the few intellectuals and the elderly. In the common view they were a sign of either the arrogance of authority or some physical weakness, hence held in some contempt. In a society that valued toughness and keenness of the senses, any sight defect could be a distinct liability for the individual and the family.

Therefore, to put the glasses on someone means showing up his or her inadequacy by comparison with someone more competent. The resulting sense of shame is meant to spur the shown-up one to greater effort.

Reckoning without the hotel keeper - Υπολογίζω χωρίς τον ξενοδόχο (Ypoloyizo horis ton xenodoho)

Meaning: failing to take basic factors into account; superficial thinking

The expression arose before the advent of modern hotels. The term *xenodoheio* originally meant an inn, or lodgement for travellers. The phrase indicates that lodgers were often unpleasantly surprised by the amount on the innkeeper's bill and may have had to alter their plans accordingly.

Saying them half - Τα λέω μισά (Ta leo misa)
Meaning: making a vague excuse; prevaricating

Someone who is unwilling to speak plainly, or admit to something openly, is often accused of saying half of what should be said. The same is conveyed in another usage, **half-words** (μισόλογα) *(misologa)*.

Shoe from your own place, even if it's patched - Παπούτσι από τον τόπο σου, κι ας είναι μπαλωμένο (Papoutsi apo ton topo sou, ki'as einai balomeno)
Meaning: one's own people and products are the best

As an example of populist chauvinism, this expression – elevated into a proverb – can hardly be bettered. The Greeks since Herodotus' day have famously considered themselves a cut above other peoples. In more modern times, wherever they have emigrated they have tended to marry within their ethnic group. Intermarriages, on the contrary, have a more than even chance of failing within a couple of years. The Greeks still feel most comfortable among themselves and have no compunctions in showing it.

Slaughtering with cotton wool - Σφάζω με το βαμβάκι (Sfazo me to vamvaki)
Meaning: condemning by kindness; the iron fist in the velvet glove

Cotton wool, at first glance, would be an unlikely instrument of murder. Yet there are ways in which it could conceivably kill. The idea here is of employing superficial kindness and smiles to demolish someone – an un-Greek trait that the Greeks somewhat enviously attribute to others, notably the English.

Stories for savages - Ιστορίες για αγρίους (Istories ya agrious)
Meaning: lame or preposterous excuses

Here lies another trace of the ancient Herodotian dichotomy between Greeks and "barbarians". It's a trace that remains firmly in the Greek psyche, resistant to present notions of political correctness that frown on the use of the word "savage" to describe

primitive people purportedly prepared to believe anything.
There is, however, an ambiguity in the Greek preposition "for", which is also translatable as "about". Thus **stories about savages** could be a synonym for fairytales.

String-sewn - Σπαγγοραμμένος (Spangorammenos)
Meaning: miser
A miser can be so miserly as to sew up his pockets with string to prevent anything from coming out of them, hence the analogy. (See **Having crabs in the pocket, p 46**)

Taking it news - Το παίρνω είδηση (To pairno eidisi)
Meaning: becoming aware of something
One of the character traits of the Greeks is that they take pride on being acutely aware of their surroundings and the world in general. They are one of Europe's more news-devouring peoples.
Saint Paul noticed this when he called at Athens in the 1st century AD. To the Greeks then as now, to be aware of the latest news was a sign of a capable and responsible intellect. Conversely, to be unaware of something, "to not take it news", was, and still is, scorned as a sign of dull-wittedness.

Tearing - Σκίζω (Skizo)
Meaning: besting someone in sports or debate
The violence of the tearing image here says something about the intensity and passion of Greek sporting contests and debates. In the third-person variant, **he/she tears** (σκίζει) *(skizei)*, the meaning is that of accomplishing something exceptionally well, thus "tearing up" the competition.
Some attribute the phrase to a runner "tearing" the ribbon at the finishing line.

The mother loses the child and the child the mother - Χάνει η μάνα το παιδί και το παιδί τη μάνα) (Hanei i mana to paidi kai to paidi ti mana)
Meaning: crowded chaos, uproar
The mother-child bond is especially strong in Greece. Therefore,

for mother and child to become separated in some confused situation, the chaos must be serious even by Greek standards. The image also carries, besides a basic lilt, a certain sound effect of women and children crying in a general brouhaha.

These are Mrs Alexander's buttons - Αυτά είναι τα κουμπιά της Αλέξαινας (Afta einai ta koumbia tis Alexainas)

Meaning: that's the essence of it

Who Mrs Alexander was and why her buttons were of such import as to end up in a deathless idiolect is an enduring mystery. What seems virtually certain is that the expression originated in the dressmaking trade. Until recently, well-to-do ladies relied heavily on dressmakers for their apparel.

Mrs Alexander may have become involved in a dispute over some luxury buttons she had ordered. Dressmakers, like other artisans, are prone to pilfering quality components and replacing them with cheaper materials. The presumed recovery of the "real" buttons, then, would have become proverbial in the dressmaking world, coming to stand for revealing the facts of a case.

The thief shouts to scare the householder - Φωνάζει ο κλέφτης να φοβηθεί ο νοικοκύρης (Fonazei o kleftis na fovithi o nikokiris)

Meaning: the aggressor pretends to be the victim.

Though this would probably be considered a proverb rather than an expression, it's colourful enough to be included here. The trait of loud self-justification is common enough in humankind. Worthy of note is the amusing mental image the phrase evokes, especially the host of associations surrounding the Greek word for householder, *nikokiris*. It's a combination of property owner, faithful family man and good money manager, an ideal of uprightness which the Greeks maintain as a totem for manliness.

To see your knickers - Να δω τα βρακιά σου (Na do ta vrakia sou)

Meaning: see if you're as brave as you think you are

One of the possible results of extreme fear is the soiling of the underwear. Another truism is that many boastful people are basically cowards. Thus, according to earthy peasant logic, the state of one's underwear would be an effective sign of that person's courage (or lack thereof) when asked to prove it.

Try and wash a black man, you waste your soap - Τον αράπη κι αν τον πλένεις, το σαπούνι σου χαλάς (Ton arapi ki'an ton pleneis, to sapouni sou halas)

Meaning: you can't change a person's nature; a leopard can't change its spots

Though this phrase (especially the English translation) may slip into politically incorrect territory, it must be stressed that Greek racism lacks the hard edge found in some other European countries and America.

The term *arapis* (equivalent to nigger) derives from Arab, which was the only dusky-skinned ethnic group the Greeks were aware of for a long time. When the first black people appeared, they were viewed with curiosity rather than hostility, perhaps because there were too few of them to stoke social opposition.

Note that the phrase itself carries no overt hostility, only a mild amusement that some people's skins may be something other than white.

Wire! - Σύρμα! (Syrma!)

Meaning: look out, the boss is coming

The probable origin of this useful codeword is the army, whose officers used to wear plenty of gold braid around sleeves and shoulders and on caps. The shiny braid could be likened to metal wire, hence the warning shout of soldiers when an officer or NCO approached and behaviour and appearance had to be brushed up within a few moments. The phrase has since seeped into civilian usage, in business and the civil service.

World and little world - Κόσμος και κοσμάκης (Kosmos kai kosmakis)

Meaning: a large and diverse crowd

The phrase could just as well be translated as "people and little people", except for the fact that the term *kosmos* in Greek means both people and world (see **It's got world**, p 17). The sense is of people high and low flocking to some public event. Public, in that otherwise the "little people", or the poor, would not be able to afford anything else.

Writing on one's old shoes - Γράφω στα παλιά μου τα παπούτσια (Grafo sta palia mou ta papoutsia)

Meaning: ignoring, treating with contempt

If the lowliest and most worn part of one's apparel is considered to be the soles of the shoes – always rubbed in the grit — then to write someone's name there is to give that person the very lowest worth. And the older the shoe, the less the worth.

The expression is a polite form of the earthier **writing on one's balls** (γράφω στ'αρχίδια μου) *(grafo st'arhidia mou)*, which ladies until recently naturally could not utter, hence the change to footwear. This variation also is of Freudian interest in treating the male genitalia as something to be ashamed of. (See **To my balls,** p 37)

In ancient Babylon the writing of one's name on the sole of a shoe was a sign of being disgraced, though the continuity with modern Greece remains unclear.

Body parts and sex

Arse and knickers - Κώλος και βρακί (Kolos kai vraki)

Meaning: inseparable

An example of two things that go together (apart from a horse and carriage) is one's underwear and the flesh it contains. The phrase is used in a derisory sense to describe two people who plot and do everything together, implying that one is under the influence of the other.

Precisely the opposite is meant by **becoming an arse** (γινόμαστε κώλος) *(yinomaste kolos)*. This phrase refers to two people whose otherwise friendly relationship is disturbed by a messy argument.

Blessing one's beard - Ευλογάω τα γένεια μου (Evlogao ta yeneia mou)
Meaning: self-praise
This sounds like a rural sideswipe at the priests, many of whom were prone to allying themselves with the rich and powerful and feathering their own nests. Any "blessings" emanating from them, therefore, were likely to be of little effect, going no farther than the priest's beard. (See **John treats, John drinks**, p 47)

Bone - Κόκκαλο (Kokkalo)
Meaning: immobile; speechless; dead
This is an example of synecdoche – the use of one characteristic of a phenomenon to stand for the whole phenomenon. The whole phenomenon in this case is death, of which a bone is a potent symbol, as in the skull and bones. Someone "remaining bone" is either someone who has died suddenly or, in a lighter context, someone intimidated into silence or compliance.

Bursting a nose - Σκάω μύτη (Skao miti)
Meaning: putting in an appearance
This expression has been known in northwest Greece for generations. It's an image from nature, namely that of tortoises and other hibernating animals that emerge in the spring, cracking the earth's crust with their noses. As one's nose is usually the first part of the body to make an appearance when entering, say, a room, the usage has a human dimension as well. It became nationally known in the mid-1990s when a feisty television game show hostess used it to call participants into camera range: "**Skase miti!**" – "Burst a nose!"

Cutting one's blood - Μου κόπηκε το αίμα (Mou kopike to aima)
Meaning: giving someone a sudden fright
Before the doctors arrived to confirm it, it was long known that a severe shock could jolt the cardiovascular system and blood circulation, "cutting" the blood flow, as it were.

Cutting one's brain - Μου κόβει το μυαλό (Mou kovei to myalo)

Meaning: becoming aware of something; seeing the light

The use of the verb to cut to denote enlightenment is associated with the sense of sharpness, as in a piercing beam of light entering the head. The Ancient Greek word for keenness of mind, *oxyderkeia,* contains the word for sharp. The phrase is most often employed in the negative sense, as in **it doesn't cut him** (δεν του κόβει) *(dhen tou kovei),* meaning that the said head is too thick for anything to penetrate it.

Cutting one's cough - Κόβω το βήχα (Kovo to viha)

Meaning: laying down the law; cutting one down to size

This is a carryover from school life, where until the 1960s or so, discipline was strict. Indolent pupils would sometimes try to mask their lack of knowledge of a particular subject by pretending to cough uncontrollably while reciting the lesson. The teacher would then threaten to "cut the cough" of the wayward student.

Cutting one's legs - Κόβονται τα πόδια (Kovontai ta podia)

Meaning: disappointment or discouragement

A person whose legs are cut cannot walk, hence the metaphor. It's used mainly in the sense of an unexpected and disappointing hindrance to one's plans.

Eat eyes' fish - Φάτε μάτια ψάρια (Fate matia psaria)

Meaning: you can look but you can't have

Another expression most likely originating in the islands, where fish has dominated the local cuisine to the point where it has become a metonym for food in general. The word-picture produced is of someone on a boat unable to catch the fish seen swimming temptingly below either because of rough weather or a lack of nets.

There could also be a medical explanation in that fish is a good source of Vitamins A and D, both good for the eyes. But this veers far from the meaning of the expression.

Eating moustaches - Τρώμε τα μουστάκια μας (Trome ta moustakia mas)

Meaning: getting into an argument

This phrase harks back to the era when any self-respecting Greek male sported a moustache. Any man engaged in a particularly acrimonious quarrel with another could be said to be opening his mouth so much and so often his moustache would be in danger of being devoured.

The expression is used among men now in a conciliatory way, such as "let's not eat our moustaches", or let's not fight over this. (See **Finding them**, p 15)

Eating one's face - Τρώω τα μούτρα μου (Troo ta moutra mou)

Meaning: coming to grief

Falling on one's face, literally or figuratively, can be likened to having "eaten", or disfigured, the features. Worthy of note is the colloquial slang word for face, *moutra,* which connotes a loss of face for the person in such a predicament.

Going bald - Καραφλιάζω (Karafliazo)

Meaning: astonishment, disbelief

Apparently arising out of the Athenian youth culture c 1980, this usage reflects the widespread view – buttressed by some medical evidence – that sudden shock can trigger drastic hair loss. The word *karafliazo* is an illiterate corruption of the correct Greek word for baldness, *falakra.*

Growing hair on the tongue - Μαλλιάζει η γλώσσα μου (Malliazei i glossa mou)

Meaning: wasting breath; talking to the wall

The expression, according to linguists, originated in Byzantine times, when over-talkative people revealing state secrets were punished by being made to chew a herb which made the tongue swell and bleed, eventually reducing the tongue surface to ribbons, hence the "hair".

There also may be some hint here of the old belief that much exercise and activity can grow hair, say, on the chest. The expression is used when by those who seek in vain to talk someone into something but end up wasting their breath.

Hairs - Τρίχες (Trihes)

Meaning: nonsense; lies

A neat, one-word dismissal of anything the speaker thinks is absurd. Why an absurdity should be likened to a hair is hard to say. There could be a clue in the variation **curly hairs** (τρίχες κατσαρές) *(trihes katsares)*, suggesting pubic hair, which is something not generally displayed in public and of not much discernible use.

He who has the beard has the combs - Όποιος έχει τα γένεια, έχει και τα χτένια (Opios ehei ta yeneia, ehei kai ta htenia)

Meaning: having the means to get oneself out of a predicament; not deserving of help

This could be a sly dig at the priesthood, who were once the only males upon whom beards were respectable. To sport a beard hence meant being a priest, hence one of the privileged and hence having the means to solve any problems they might have without much public sympathy.

Homosexual-like - Πούστικα (Poustika)

Meaning: double-crossing

Despite homosexuality having been accepted socially in ancient Greece, it has taken a long time for the modern Greek gay to dare to come out. The colloquial and disparaging term for a male homosexual is *poustis,* a corruption of the Turkish *pusht*. In less permissive times to deceive or double-cross someone, to be not what one seemed, was to act like a homosexual, ie seeming to be one thing but in reality being another.

Interestingly, the term *poustis* remains a highly useful multi-purpose word. It can be a mock-abusive term of friendly address common among men both straight and gay, and even now among women. It can also be a term of real abuse in the appropriate situation. A particularly disliked politician, a surly traffic policeman or taxi driver, a short-changing shopkeeper or some such petty crook, all can come under the *poustis* category independently of sexual orientation.

The plosive *p* at the beginning, like the beginning of a spit, makes the word particularly satisfying to utter loudly and accusingly. (The equivalent for females would be *poutana,* or whore – another word with a good loud *p* at the beginning.)

Knife to the bone - Μαχαίρι στο κόκκαλο (Mahairi sto kokkalo)

Meaning: getting to the bottom of something; a strict rendering of justice

Here is a medical metaphor of cutting out the rot from a living organism, which in surgical terms often means reaching to the bone. The expression, much uttered by politicians and the media, is honoured more in the breach than in the observance.

Like the iris of the eye - Σαν κόρη οφθαλμού (San kori ofthalmou)

Meaning: keeping safe

When Greeks mention something of extreme value that has to be safeguarded come what may, they liken it to the iris of the eye, the part of that organ most vitally connected with sight, hence the most valuable.

Making a belly - Κάνω κοιλιά (Kano kilia)

Meaning: flagging in interest

The phrase is used most often to describe a film or play or book whose interest begins to wane at some point in the middle. The basic image is that of a clothesline that makes a curve when weighed down by clothes. It could also have something to do with the belly that many men acquire in middle age as their life loses the plot somewhere.

Making black eyes - Κάνω μαύρα μάτια (Kano mavra matia)

Meaning: missing someone from not having seen them for a long time

We see here that the term "black eye" in Greek is very different from its English meaning! In the context of the sombre overtones that the colour black carries in the psyche, a black eye is an eye that has mourned (figuratively worn black) the long absence of some person, such as a lover or fond relative.

May your mouth be sanctified - Να αγιάσει το στόμα σου (Na ayiasei to stoma sou)

Meaning: well-said; hear, hear

The divinity of saints has always loomed large over the Greeks' spiritual life. So it would seem natural that when something is uttered that stands out from the usual cant and hypocrisy, especially when an injustice is pointed out, the hearer would invoke saintly blessings upon the speaker of truth.

A variation on the same theme is **from your mouth to the ears of God** (από το στόμα σου στου Θεού τ'αυτί) *(apo to stoma sou stou Theou t'afti)*, voicing a devout wish that something uttered might come to pass.

Medicine-tongue - Φαρμακόγλωσσα) (Farmakoglossa)

Meaning: a venomous tongue; sarcastic person

In some parts of Greece the term for medicine is the same as that for poison, an echo of a time when the two were largely indistinguishable. The female version, arguably more common, is *farmakoglossi*.

Some men employ a similar term, **medicine-vagina** (φαρμακομούνα) *(farmakomouna)*, to describe a woman who has been widowed more than once, and hence to be avoided like the plague. The feeling is that for multiple husbands to have died, her vagina must contain some "poison".

My fats, my charms - Τα πάχη μου, τα κάλλη μου (Ta pahi mou, ta kalli mou)

Meaning: a fat woman is more attractive than a thin one.

Rake-thin Western ladies, take note. In a largely rural and poor society, largeness in woman has been the *par excellence* sign of health and robustness, and above all, child-bearing endurance. The present bony fashion model ideal would not have lasted long in the fields and farms and fishing boats. The emphasis on child-bearing capacity was understandable in an insecure society where disease and war were rampant. Even now, in country areas, the plump wife is afforded huge social respect.

Not filling the eye - Δεν γεμίζει το μάτι (Den yemizei to mati)

Meaning: not making much of an impression
When vision is focused on something less than impressive, it lacks "fullness" or satisfaction. The phrase is commonly used to describe perceived personal failings, for example, the flimsy attributes of a prospective son-in-law or daughter-in-law from a critical parent's point of view.

Of the whore - Της πουτάνας (Tis poutanas)

Meaning: chaotic, in a state of uproar
Most likely a city expression, originating in Athens or the pre-1922 cosmopolitan Greek cities of Asia Minor. Red-light districts in large cities naturally attract characters prone to brawling and mayhem in competition for a good-looking prostitute or in a quarrel over the revenue. "Of the whore" could also mean "at the whore's place", which in days gone by would often have been a disorderly place. (See **Of the madwoman**, p 19)

A recent variation (first heard in the 1970s) is **of the whore's railing** (της πουτάνας το κάγκελο) *(tis poutanas to kangelo)*. Brothels never were the best-maintained places, so this phrase is probably an echo of some hapless patron who fell from a brothel balcony when a railing broke, resulting naturally in some degree of uproar.

One's ear not sweating - Δεν ιδρώνει το αυτί μου (Den idronei to afti mou)

Meaning: ignoring; being impervious to pleas
When someone refuses to heed an urgent request or see an important point, the suggestion is that one's ear has not done enough work – has not "sweated" – to take in the needed information. The phrase is much used as a criticism of haughty public officials impervious to the problems of the populace.

One's head a cauldron - Το κεφάλι καζάνι (To kefali kazani)

Meaning: giddy from overwork or too much noise
A cauldron full of water is heavy, and the water boils when

heated, which is an accurate description of one's head when fatigued or being on the receiving end of the wife's harangue.

One's tongue a necktie - Η γλώσσα γραβάτα (I glossa gravata)
Meaning: thirsty; hot and exhausted
This is a recent (c 1980) addition to the roster of Greek idiolects. Besides the cartoonishly humorous image it projects of a tongue hanging out, it assonates and alliterates pleasantly in Greek – and in flawless iambic feet at that. Hence it deserves its place in the roster.

Out of the teeth - Έξω απ' τα δόντια (Exo ap'ta dontia)
Meaning: outspokenly; calling a spade a spade
This usage arguably goes back to Homer, in whose *Iliad* the imprecation "what is this that has escaped the fence of your teeth?" is often found. The teeth symbolize the last barrier to the emergence of speech, after which what is said cannot be taken back. The phrase is thus also used to denote a "telling it like it is", uncaring of the reaction. (See **Calling figs figs and a basin a basin,** p 41)

Paying the hairs of one's head - Πληρώνω τα μαλλιά της κεφαλής μου (Plirono ta mallia tis kefalis mou)
Meaning: paying a lot of money, more than something is worth
Most likely this is a reference to the number of hairs on one's head, when translated into monetary terms, signifying "a lot". Also, when all one's possessions and clothes are gone, the only easily removable parts of the body are one's hairs.

Playing on the fingers - Παίζω στα δάχτυλά μου (Paizo sta dahtyla mou)
Meaning: displaying high ability or expertise
The agility of the fingers is a good metaphor for any kind of skill, manual or mental. The suggestion here is that of mastering something, such as a puppet's strings or piano keys. People, by extension, can also be thus "played" as well.

Putting two feet in one shoe - Βάζω τα δύο πόδια σ' ένα παπούτσι (Vazo ta dyo podia s'ena papoutsi)

Meaning: taking control; putting someone in their place

Placing both feet into one shoe is the ultimate image of restriction and disciplining. Feminists love this phrase, often used by strong-headed young women who vow to tame their wayward men in this hobbling fashion once they get them to the altar.

Shit inside - Χέσε μέσα (Hese mesa)

Meaning: forget it; it's a disaster

No elaborate explanation is required here, as the act of defecating into something other than the proper receptacle would make that something quite abominable and best abandoned. The phrase – always employed in the imperative – is a telling example of the Greeks' gleeful use of semi-obscenity to make a point.

Shitting them - Τα σκατώνω (Ta skatono)

Meaning: making a mess of something

Since to defecate on something (see previous entry) is to render it particularly useless, the image is particularly effective, if not yet fully accepted by polite society.

Swallowing the tongue - Καταπίνω τη γλώσσα μου (Katapino ti glossa mou)

Meaning: being rendered speechless or proved wrong

To the voluble Greeks the tongue and its use have been vital throughout their history. As in English, the word tongue in Greek is a synonym and metonym at the same time for language. Hence, swallowing one's tongue, that is, gulping in embarrassment, is to momentarily lack the power of speech.

Taking an eye out - Βγάζει μάτι (Vgazei mati)

Meaning: dropping a clanger; jarring

To the Greek, the eye has always had supreme importance. Perhaps it's because of the sharp Greek sunlight, which could well have influenced the great ancient sculptors and artists. In

Christian times God was represented on many church doors as a great eye surveying all. It may not be going too far to say that the Greek, the inhabitant of the sunniest land in Europe, is a sight freak. Thus something that jars, either visually or otherwise, is equivalent to an eye being poked out.

Taking it on the skull - Τα παίρνω στο κρανίο (Ta pairno sto kranio)
Meaning: being astonished, dumfounded, angry
The derivation here is fairly self-explanatory. The phrase emerged from the 1990s youth culture and spread rapidly to all age groups. (See **The sky coming a distaff**, p 60)

Taking one's tail out - Βγάζω την ουρά μου απ'έξω (Vgazo tin oura mou ap'exo)
Meaning: evading responsibility; making excuses
Here is an image from the animal world. In cats and dogs, the tail is the part of the body most vulnerable to being trapped or trodden on. Gathering up the tail, then, is a way of avoiding possible injury. In human terms, the phrase denotes a certain cowardice, an avoidance of the onus of responsibility for something.

Taking on one's neck - Παίρνω στο λαιμό μου (Pairno sto laimo mou)
Meaning: causing the misfortune of another
As in English, the term neck has become synonymous with life, as an exceptionally vulnerable part of the human body. The phrase has come to mean sending someone to undeserved punishment through one's own sins. It can also be likened to the sense of an albatross of guilt around one's neck.

Tangling our thighs - Μπλέκουμε τα μπούτια μας (Blekoume ta boutia mas)
Meaning: getting involved in a confusing dispute or conflict of interest
The expression is almost always used in the past tense first person plural, ie "we tangled our thighs." A sexual connotation can be discerned in the image. Therefore the phrase could have

arisen out of a love affair gone sour, a once-passionate melding of bodies degenerating into a mere awkward tangling of limbs.

The out-of-here - Τον εξαποδώ (Ton ex'apodo)

Meaning: cancer; the devil

Older people still have the tendency to refuse to utter the name of potentially fatal diseases such as cancer, as if by some sinister power their very utterance would bring the feared malady into the house. It's a probable relic of the old and pervasive fear of witchcraft, which explains the use of the term among old women to signify the devil.

To my balls - Στ' αρχίδια μου (St'arhidia mou)

Meaning: I don't give a damn

As Mediterraneans, the Greeks have been largely spared the severer religio-cultural hangups over body parts and sexual functions. The ancient Greeks had no qualms about exhibiting the nude male form, for example, in the appropriate public setting. The modern Greek male remains sensitively proud of his standard reproductive equipment.

So, it may be asked, why this derogatory usage of *arhidia* (stemming from the ancient form *orheis*) in more recent times? Christianity undoubtedly played its part in stemming the more egregious elements of Greek nudity and pagan licence. But it fails to explain why a highly important part of the male body should be so demoted, indeed, as to be a synonym for something of no consequence, or item of poor quality. Here is a task for a psycho-linguist.

As in other languages, the Freudian preoccupation with sex and its instruments has fixed its terms high on the list of spoken colloquialisms. In Greece there is also a lesser-used equivalent of the expression featuring the corresponding portion of the female anatomy. But in more recent times women in their own speech have come to almost universally employ the male version, illogically - yet effectively - in terms of symbolic female empowerment.

Welcome my two eyes - Καλώς τα μάτια μου τα δυό (Kalos ta matia mou ta dyo)

Meaning: happy to see you; you are most welcome

A soppily affectionate greeting, probably originating in the Aegean islands or Cyprus, that has nonetheless come to carry a condescending tone, as in an adult to a child. It remains primarily a women's expression.

However, there exists an obscene variant once beloved of adolescent boys, uttered *sotto voce* upon the arrival of an unpopular teacher: **welcome my two balls** (καλώς τ' αρχίδια μου τα δυό) *(kalos t'arhidia mou ta dyo).*

Words of the arse - Λόγια του κώλου (Logia tou kolou)

Meaning: silly, worthless or exaggerated utterances

The analogy with the passing of wind is here apparent. There is also the common use of the backside image to connote ridicule or inferiority.

The Greek word for backside *(kolos)* is a direct descendant of the ancient *kolon,* which has passed down into universal medical usage as *colon.* In Modern Greek it has altered its original anatomic sense to mean the buttocks. Its negative connotation remains strong, as in the related term *kolopaido,* literally arse-boy, or an ill-mannered, delinquent youth.

Your eyes fourteen - Τα μάτια σου δεκατέσσερα (Ta matia sou dekatessera)

Meaning: keep your eyes open, your wits about you.

The phrase is an enhancement of "your eyes four" *(ta matia sou tessera)* that befits an insecure society such as Greece was for most of its mediaeval and modern period, when public institutions were weak or nonexistent. It's the dictum of rugged individualism: the ubiquitous foe or rival is always out there, and one must be self-reliant and watchful in an often menacing world.

Scholars believe that it originated on the island of Chios in Ottoman times. It was said that if a Turk saw a Greek walking alone, he had the right to ask the Greek to carry him on his back. Thus in Chios people tended to walk in pairs. So if they met a Turk in the street, one of the Greeks carried the other on his back to avoid being pressed into service. As pairs of Greeks were constantly on the lookout for Turks, between them they had four eyes.

Animals, plants and food

A bad dog doesn't die - Κακό σκυλί ψόφο δεν έχει (Kako skyli psofo den ehei)
Meaning: bad people seem to live longer than others
This phrase expresses a common complaint of humankind, going back eons, known to the Hebrew psalmists as well as the Greek tragedians. One explanation could be that "bad" people give vent to their innate disagreeableness more often, or are simply not as hypocritical as the rest of us, therefore avoiding the bodily ills associated with emotional repression.

A cuckoo costing a nightingale - Στοιχίζει ο κούκος αηδόνι (Stihizei o koukos aidoni)
Meaning: overpaying, being overcharged
In terms of the pecking order of birds, it seems that the cuckoo is of a lower order than a nightingale. Paying for a nightingale and getting a cuckoo, then, is seen as being the victim of a bad deal.

A donkey bursts - Σκάει γάιδαρος (Skaei gaidaros)
Meaning: it's stiflingly hot
The donkey, a hardy Mediterranean beast, is known for its adaptability to hot weather. So if a donkey is in imaginary danger of bursting, it must be hot indeed. There is also **the cicada bursts** (σκάει ο τζίτζικας) *(skaei o tzitzikas),* with the same sense of heat, this time overwhelming even the chirping hot-weather insect.

Also, someone who tries people's patience can be said to "make a donkey burst", an apt analogy as the donkey is the most patient of beasts.

Bean bean, the bag fills - Φασούλι το φασούλι, γεμίζει το σακούλι (Fasouli to fasouli, yemizei to sakouli)
  Meaning: saving a little at a time brings prosperity
  This is another scarcity saying, equivalent to the English "take care of the pence and the pounds will take care of themselves". A smart peasant, by saving a bean at a time, eventually would have a full bag of them. A good lesson in frugality (and rhyming to boot), it is for that reason not very popular in a modern consumerist society.

Becoming a gnat - Γίνομαι σκνίπα (Yinomai sknipa)
  Meaning: getting blind drunk
  Someone who is too drunk to drive, walk or even utter a coherent sentence can be said to have the mental powers of the smallest of insects, or be as helpless as a gnat when trapped in a light.

Becoming balls of wool - Γίνομαι μαλλιά-κουβάρια (Yinomai mallia kouvaria)
  Meaning: getting involved in a bitter dispute
  There is a touch of fur flying in this image. The reference to balls of wool places the phrase in the female camp, suggesting irate women interrupting their knitting to hurl balls of wool at each other.

Becoming leaf and feather - Γίνεται φύλλο και φτερό (Yinetai fyllo kai ftero)
  Meaning: disintegrating, being torn to pieces
  The expression is often used as a cliche to describe a home or shop that has been burgled and vandalised. It suggests an origin in a bloody encounter in nature, with the leaf a metonym for broken foliage and the feather standing for the remains of a bird.

Being a cat - Είμαι γάτα (Eimai gata)
  Meaning: being crafty, cunning, astute
  The Greeks share few, if any, of the cuddly-pet associations

that the cat has, for example, among the English. Greek cats have been, and remain, hardier beasts, the survivors of centuries of neglect and abuse by farmers and householders who saw them only as mouse-catching machines, inherently dirty and barely fit for human cohabitation.

A cat in Greek carries distinct connotations of slyness, self-calculation and quick-wittedness, all key feline traits. Thus a man who "is a cat" has the respected ability to survive in politics or business, though he's not exactly a well-loved figure in society.

Boil rice - Βράσε ρύζι (Vrase rizi)

Meaning: fat chance; it's not going to happen

Like most food metaphors in Greek colloquialisms, this one harks back to pre-mid-20th century times when food was scarce among large sections of the rural population. Meat was considered a rare luxury. Cheap vegetarian dishes were the norm. The phrase "boil rice" signifies that as it would be delusional to expect meat at any ordinary mealtime, simpler fare such as rice would have to do.

It was, and is, uttered in a cynical mode, together with the characteristic gesture of making a circular motion with the right hand. Another version employing the Ancient Greek word for rice, *vrase oryza,* is also used, to bring out the cynical element even more.

Calling figs figs and a basin a basin - Λέω τα σύκα σύκα και τη σκάφη σκάφη (Leo ta sika sika kai ti skafi skafi)

Meaning: plain talking; calling a spade a spade

The image here is culled from autumn fig-harvesting time, when the squishy green fruit is plucked off the trees and gathered in baskets or basins. One might well imagine some attempt at trickery during the weighing, as in the basin being weighed along with the figs. To separate the two would be a sign of honest dealing. Hence the connotation of plain-talking frankness.

Careful the eggs - Σιγά τ'αυγά (Siga t'avga)

Meaning: big deal

Someone carrying eggs must needs be careful with them. In

times when eggs were a luxury, transporting them required especial care. The expression comes into play when someone makes an exaggerated fuss about something trivial, or displays some ludicrous self-importance. (See **Careful the chandelier,** p 63)

Catching birds in midair - Πιάνω πουλιά στον αέρα (Piano poulia ston aera)

Meaning: being unusually clever and/or agile

Another phrase arguably harking back to Homeric times where sheer prowess in anything was the supreme human quality. Catching a bird in midair would indeed betoken a godlike quality which all Greek males still secretly believe to be theirs.

The caught animal can vary. For a real challenge, one might seize a flea in midflight **(piano psillo ston aera).** And for the indecent, the verb to catch may be replaced by the basic sexual one.

Catching in the leeks - Πιάνω στα πράσα (Piano sta prassa)

Meaning: catching red-handed

In an agricultural society petty theft was usually confined to filching crops from a neighbour's field. Leeks were an especially valued crop, as they could be made into a nourishing soup, and hence prone to theft. Anyone caught in someone else's leeks was thus a serious troublemaker.

Doing the dead bug - Κάνω τον ψόφιο κοριό (Kano ton psofio korio)

Meaning: feigning sleep; avoiding attention

Dead insects usually lie on their backs with their legs in the air. Live human beings wishing to imitate them are deemed to have something to hide. The expression is aimed at those who guiltily shrink out of sight, or feign sleep or illness, in the face of accusations.

Doing the duck - Κάνω την πάπια (Kano tin papia)

Meaning: remaining unobtrusive, not rocking the boat

The duck, one of the less noisy members of the ornithological kingdom, is here used as a symbol of quiescence. Yet as the Greeks as a national character are far from quiescent, such untypical behaviour is almost invariably deemed to have some ulterior motive. Deliberately playing the fool or not rocking the boat in a potentially difficult situation is one of them.

A Greek thus "does the duck" not out of timidity but as a tactical manoeuvre. Not a few historians are prepared to argue that such tactics helped the Greeks stay together as a nation through aeons of alien rule.

Delousing - Ψειρίζω (Pseirizo)

Meaning: nitpicking; paying too much attention to detail

One of the commoner pastimes of poor peasant mothers was to spend hours picking lice and fleas out of their children's hair. It was a painstaking operation, and ultimately futile in that the vermin would soon reappear.

Eating one's horns - Τρώω τα κέρατά μου (Troo ta kerata mou)

Meaning: eating overmuch

In a country that historically was not rich in food resources, feasts such as weddings and saint's days were occasions for enjoying that greatest of luxuries, meat. As all red meat except pork derives from horned beasts, eating the horns as well would indicate an excessive appetite.

Something else briefly intrudes. The phrase "one's horns" could possibly signal a reference to cuckoldry. If there is such a connection, it must be extremely tenuous. (See **Eating the curtain, p 44**)

Eating someone - Τον τρώω / τον έφαγα (Ton troo / ton efaga)

Meaning: getting the better of someone

In a poor and insecure society there are few qualms about how to obtain food. Being able to outwit the other person in the struggle for survival becomes a real social virtue which today is expressed, for example, in grabbing a parking space before the driver in front can back into it. "He's eaten it from me," *(Mou to'fage)* exclaims the driver cheated out of his parking. "I ate him!" *(Ton efaga)* gloats the other, I've bested the next guy.

A variation is **eating someone cabbage** (τον τρώω λάχανο) *(ton troo lahano)*, emphasising the sweetness of such an illegitimate victory. In the Greek cuisine, cabbage with olive oil and lemon makes a succulent summer salad.

Conjecture that the eating reference is a distant echo of a prehistoric cannibal society must remain just that – conjecture.

Eating stupid grass - Τρώω κουτόχορτο (Troo koutohorto)

Meaning: gullible, being taken for a fool

The phrase evokes the image of a dull-eyed chewing of cud by sheep and goats. But there is strong evidence that the term *koutohorto* actually refers to hashish, smoked in the dens of Piraeus in the early 20th century and helping give rise to that deadening brand of bouzouki music called *rembetika*. Hashish is, after all, a weed that stupefies.

Eating the curtain - Τρώω το καταπέτασμα (Troo to katapetasma)

Meaning: ravenous gluttony

Hunger was such a constant presence in the rural Greece of old that the appearance of good food often provoked uncontrolled eating – to the point at which, in this expression – not even the curtains were spared.

Fleas entering the ear - Μπαίνουν ψύλλοι στ' αυτιά (Bainoun psylli st'aftia)

Meaning: having a sneaking suspicion

When fleas enter a Greek ear their effect is quite different from that in an English ear. To have a flea in one's ear in English is to be irritated over something; in Greek it's to become suspicious. The fleas here stand for those little suspicions or intuitions that something is amiss entering the mind and not going away. In Greece, at least, they seem to turn out to be largely justified. Some attribute the usage to the time of the Byzantine emperor Julian the Apostate, who is said to have punished plotters and eavesdroppers by putting fleas in their ears.

For a flea's jump - Για ψύλλου πήδημα (Yia psyllou pidima)

Meaning: for the most trivial of reasons; at the drop of a hat

In Greece's warm climate fleas used to be more common than they are now. Anyone familiar with this creature knows that it jumps at the slightest stimulus. The phrase is most often used for someone who takes offence at the slightest provocation. Incidentally, having a flea jumping all over one is not calculated to engender peace of mind.

Getting the olive oil out of one - Βγάζω το λάδι (Vgazo to ladi)

Meaning: becoming exhausted; exasperating someone

The image here is from the olive oil press which crushes the olives in a hopper to produce the vital fluid. The expression is mostly used in the first person past tense such as **[he/she] got the olive oil out of me** to denote a mixture of exhaustion and exasperation.

Getting the snake out of the hole - Βγάζω το φίδι απ' την τρύπα (Vgazo to fidi ap'tin tripa)

Meaning: handling a tricky situation; pulling the chestnuts out of the fire

Attempting to dispose of a snake threatening one's livestock by drawing it out of its hole used to be one of the more hazardous, yet necessary, tasks of rural life. In modern usage, the phrase is used whenever someone is forced into a socially unpopular act when others shirk it, such as the need to deliver bad news.

Green horses - Πράσιν' άλογα (Prasin' aloga)

Meaning: nonsense; absurdities

Scholars perk up at this usage, which they claim is an "acoustic orthography", in other words an exact soundalike of the Ancient Greek phrase πράσσειν άλογα *(prassein aloga),* meaning to act unreasonably, or nonsensically.

Having crabs in the pocket - Έχω καβούρια στην τσέπη μου) (Eho kavouria stin tsepi mou)

Meaning: being miserly; not wanting to spend money

The reference to crabs most likely harks back to an island or maritime origin. The image is well-crafted. Having your pocket crawling with crabs would make you rather reluctant to put your hand in it. The Greeks, though traditionally poor, have always held generosity to be a cardinal virtue and, correspondingly, hold parsimony in contempt. Hence the dour humour of the image.

Having eaten one's breads - Έφαγε τα ψωμιά του (Efage ta psomia tou)

Meaning: dead or at death's door; having had one's chips

This is one way of joking about death and thus attempting to come to terms with it. There comes a day, after all, when you eat no more bread. The term "bread" is, of course, also a metonym for food. The phrase is always employed in the third person past tense, ie "he's had his breads," with naturally no fear that the person so referred to will take it amiss.

He who is hungry dreams of loaves - Όποιος πεινάει, καρβέλια ονειρεύεται (Opios pinaei karvelia oneirevetai)

Meaning: indulging in wishful thinking

This is a full-fledged proverb rather than an expression, included here for its evidence of origin in a society where a whole loaf of bread was a luxury. It's also psychologically meaningful as a description of the subconscious dream process. The noun *oneiro,* meaning to dream, also means to daydream.

Home-cat - Σπιτόγατος (Spitogatos)

Meaning: a stay-at-home; a lazy, introverted person

The image of the cat curled up in front of the fireplace, oblivious to the world, would ring true in English, which makes its appearance in Greek all the more odd. The Greek image of the cat has never been particularly benign (see **Being a cat,** p 40). The use of the term for tomcat *(-gatos)* is even odder, as tomcats don't usually sit quietly at home. For the expression to make semantic sense, the connotation is of a tomcat sitting at home out of sheer indifferent laziness, which among Greek human beings is a socially undesirable trait.

John treats, John drinks - Γιάννης κερνάει, Γιάννης πίνει (Yannis kernaei, Yannis pinei)

Meaning: doing something ostensibly for others but really for oneself.

The use of John (Yannis) as a generic name for all men (as once in English) indicates that the name was even more common among Greeks than it is now.

Greek social manners remain heavily influenced by Ottoman practice. Treating someone to a drink or a meal – not easy in times of poverty – signifies selflessness and nobility of spirit. To turn such an act into a self-serving one would be in such poor taste as to leave its mark on a special idiolect. (See **Blessing one's beard,** p 27)

Life and hen - Ζωή και κότα (Zoi kai kota)

Meaning: prosperity; the good life

As a people with a history of poverty and insecurity, the Greeks have never been plagued with that vague guilt that accompanies material wealth in Protestant climes. The good life is to be sought after avidly, even by illegal means, and bully for him who manages it. The "hen" in the expression is probably a reference to roast chicken as a dish indicative of a certain level of luxury. The hen could also refer to the presence of a woman, making happiness complete.

Life is a cucumber - Η ζωή είναι αγγούρι (I zoi einai angouri)

Meaning: life is full of problems

The humble cucumber shares with the banana the dubious distinction of being the unavoidable phallic image. The cucumber is thus true to its semantic function in this expression, as something that can invade, or violate, one's sense of well-being.

Like the dog in the vineyard - Σαν το σκυλί στ'αμπέλι (San to skyli st' ambeli)

Meaning: meaninglessly; in sordid circumstances

This phrase is almost always used to describe a miserable or tragically avoidable death. In pastoral times, a strange dog seen prowling in a vineyard or other economically useful property such as a flock of hens could expect to be shot on sight. The dog's death would thus become an example of something pointless or sordid. The expression is most often used to apply to human beings who come to a bad end through questionable morals or criminal association.

Live, May, to eat clover - Ζήσε Μάη μου, να φας τριφύλλι (Zise Mai mou, na fas trifylli)

Meaning: you'll wait for ever

The only sure thing than can be said about this particularly abstruse text is that it must be agricultural in origin. Greek farmers still plant clover in crop-exhausted fields to replenish the soil nutrients. Clover reaches maturity in the late spring, hence the reference to May. When harvested and dried it's a valuable winter fodder for livestock, which may account for its place of honour in a vernacular phrase. Drawing the bow for a very long shot, the sense seems to be that May must wait until winter — ie a long time — until the clover becomes edible.

There is some disagreement over whether "May" *(Mai)* is a corruption of "black" in the vocative declension *(mavre)*. The phrase would then be **live, my black one, to eat clover** (Ζήσε, μαύρε, να φας τριφύλλι) *(Zise, mavre, na fas trifylli)*. This, in the alternative explanation, would be what is said to a black horse to be patient until the spring, when he can eat fresh clover.

Not a flea on the back of your neck - Ούτε ψύλλος στον κόρφο σου (Oute psyllos ston korfo sou)

Meaning: your reputation is intact; you are beyond criticism

In the days when washing was relatively infrequent, many of the poorer people were infested with fleas. Thus if, say, a peasant were to go into town for a haircut, fleas on the back of his neck would betray a certain uncouthness. A flealess neck, on the other hand, would be a sign of cleanliness.

Not chewing - Δεν μασάω (Den masao)

Meaning: don't give me that; I don't believe you

This is a relatively new (probably mid-1990s) addition to the rich trove of Greek idiolects from the youth culture. It's too early to tell whether it will have any staying power, though there are signs that it's already becoming *demode* in the Athenian cafe circuit. The link between taking in dubious information and refusing to chew dubious food is obvious.

One on the nail and one on the horseshoe - Μια στο καρφί και μια στο πέταλο (Mia sto karfi kai mia sto petalo)

Meaning: scoring argumental points; driving the message home

We are no authority on the art of blacksmithing, but it seems reasonable to assume that a shoer of horses, to affix the shoe more firmly to the hoof, would hammer not only the nail but the shoe metal itself – presumably to provide some extra insurance against the shoe coming off.

Promising hares with surplices - Τάζω λαγούς με πετραχείλια (Tazo lagous me petraheilia)

Meaning: wild promises, difficult or impossible to keep

The hare is a rural image; the surplice an ecclesiastical one. Their juxtaposition might seem odd unless it is remembered that the two environments were always closely tied. The picture of a hare wearing a priestly vestment, as an image of absurdity, must have been comical enough to ensure its durability.

Pumpkin drums - Κολοκύθια τούμπανα (Kolokythia toumbana)

Meaning: nonsense; hot air

An overripe pumpkin gradually dries up, eventually leaving a hard outer shell over a sac of air. Thus the Greeks say the vegetable "has become a drum" *(toumbaniase)* – that is, little more than air.

Putting water in one's wine - Βάζω νερό στο κρασί μου (Vazo nero sto krasi mou)

Meaning: changing one's previously extreme position

This is an echo of the sensible ancient Greek practice of watering wine to lessen the possibility of inebriation, especially while carrying out philosophical debates (as in Plato's *Symposium*). It was a key technique of Socrates to force his debating adversaries into logically untenable positions, compelling them to modify, or "water down", their arguments.

Roasting a fish on the lips - Ψήνω το ψάρι στα χείλη (Psino to psari sta heili)

Meaning: making one suffer for one's misdeeds

The image defies rational analysis. The closest one can get is to assume that the red face of a contrite, guilt-stricken person would be hot enough to roast a fish on (the fish being perhaps a sign of island origin). The burning lips could be reference to lying words that are being paid for by having something cooked on them. The phrase is generally used only by vengeful women intent on, or boasting of, punishing their wayward men (see **Putting two feet into one shoe**, p 35). Some authorities claim that the phrase arises out of a peculiar form of monastic punishment.

Say hello to the plane tree - Χαιρέτα μας τον πλάτανο (Haireta mas ton platano)

Meaning: you're unrealistic; it'll never happen

In many, if not most, Greek villages the main square is the centre of social life. More often than not, the squares are shaded by immense plane trees, offering a temptation to sit under one with a beer in hand and to switch off for the day, especially in summer.

He who lolls under a plane tree is likely to be in a dreamy, semi-inebriated or semi-conscious state, and thus prone to making unrealistic or drunken statements. To a sober observer it may seem as if he's talking, or saying hello, to the plane tree.

Sitting on one's eggs - Κάθομαι σ' αυγά μου (Kathomai st'avga mou)

Meaning: sitting still; minding one's own business

This is an image taken from rural life, where a broody hen sitting on her eggs is the supreme example of not being meddlesome. **Sit on your eggs** (Κάτσε στ' αυγά σου) *(Katse st'avga sou)* is a common way of saying stay out of it.

Sleeping with the hens - Κοιμάμαι με τις κότες (Kimamai me tis kotes)
Meaning: going to bed early
Early to bed and early to rise never has been a maxim of the Greeks, who readily stay up till all hours and put their children through the same ordeal. Thus going to bed early to get adequate rest is seen as wimpish behaviour, reminiscent of the hens in the coop which shut their eyes at sundown.

Stinging them - Τα τσούζω (Ta tsouzo)
Meaning: drinking heavily
The phrase is more often used to describe the alcoholic rather than the social drinker, and refers more to whisky and other hard beverages than to beer and wine. "Them" refers to the number of glasses drunk, while the "stinging" is the smarting, burning sensation of potent liqueur going down the throat. (See **Becoming a gnat, p 40)**

The dappled goat laughs - Γελάει το παρδαλό κατσίκι (Yelaei to pardalo katsiki)
Meaning: this is ludicrous
It's similar to the English "making a cat laugh" with a different animal protagonist, one more closely tied to Greek rural society. Why a goat should be dappled to illustrate the hilarity of any given situation is open to conjecture. Perhaps a dappled goat has more of a clownish appearance.

Linguists offer a more historical explanation. The first recorded use of the phrase, they say, was in a newspaper in 1945. A cartoonist of the time drew a striped or dappled goat to personify a particularly unpopular government minister.

The fava has a hole in it - Κάποιο λάκκο έχει η φάβα (Kapio lakko ehei i fava)
Meaning: there's a catch somewhere; things aren't what they seem

Fava is the yellow, polenta-like paste made by boiling and crushing the fava bean. It's one of those staple peasant foods that has sustained generations and these days is served in tavernas as an appetiser that goes well with olive oil and onion.

A plate of fava should present a smooth surface without being watery. But in badly cooked fava, air bubbles may lurk beneath the surface. Thus the sense is that a certain situation is not what it seems to be.

There's Rhodes, there's the jump - Ιδού η Ρόδος, ιδού το πήδημα (Idou i Rodos, idou to pidima)

Meaning: keep your promise; put your money where your mouth is

One of Aesop's fables tells of an Athenian athlete who sailed to Rhodes to take part in a footrace there. The runner was known to be a bit of a braggart, so when he returned to Athens his claims of accomplishment were taken with a grain of salt. Whereupon one of his friends drew a line in the dust, wrote "Rhodes" next to it and told the athlete to jump over it – "there's Rhodes, there's the jump." Realising that the mickey was being taken out of him, the runner slunk away in shame.

The wood chipping will burn - Θα καεί το πελεκούδι (Tha kaei to pelekoudi)

Meaning: we'll have a roaring good time

Before the advent of television and nightclubs, having a good time in rural Greece meant gathering round a blazing wood fire and singing songs and drinking until dawn. On festive occasions such as weddings and saint's days, all the wood chippings gathered from the woodpile would be thrown into the fire, stoking it yet more.

To the roast - Στο ψητό (Sto psito)

Meaning: to the heart of the matter

In a food-conscious society the heart of every meal is (ideally, at least) the roast meat entree. Getting straight to the roast is thus an apposite metaphor for getting directly to the heart of an issue.

Tough glass - Γερό ποτήρι (Yero potiri)

Meaning: a prolific drinker

The glass of wine is here employed as a metaphor for the habit of drinking, much as, for example, a table stands for food (see **Making a table**, p 18). A tough glass carries a respectful connotation. He or she is one who can drink a lot without the stigma of being an alcoholic, for which other, more negative, terms come into play. (See **Becoming a gnat** and **Stinging them**, pp 40, 51)

Wanting both the pie and the dog well-fed - Θέλουμε και την πίτα ολόκληρη και το σκύλο χορτάτο (Theloume kai tin pitta olokliri kai to skylo hortato)

Meaning: wanting it both ways; having one's cake and eating it, too

Before the city habit of keeping pets became common, rural animals were not especially well-fed or treated. Where food was concerned, the people would have the pie and the dog the scraps. Therefore, feeding both people and beast adequately became a metaphor for mutually exclusive alternatives.

We ate the ox, its tail remains - Φάγαμε το βόιδι, η ουρά έμεινε (Fagame to voidi, i oura emeine)

Meaning: giving up just before reaching one's goal

Another saying right out of pastoral life. Roast ox was a substantial meal. Though there is no record of the Greeks ever eating oxtail soup, to give up at the tail when the whole carcass had gone would indicate a last-minute failure of willpower.

Whatever we eat, whatever we drink and whatever our arse grabs - Ό,τι φάμε, ό,τι πιούμε κι ό,τι αρπάξει ο κώλος μας (Oti fame, oti pioume ki oti arpaxei o kolos mas)

Meaning: take your pleasures while you can; live for the day

The light-heartedness and mild obscenity of this expression mask its ultimate despair and alienation, inevitable products of a materialist society and stifling city life. It's a paean to pessimism, noticeably lacking that wry humour that marks those of rural origin.

The term arse *(kolos)* here is a crude synonym for the male and female genitalia, thus in one word including the pleasures of the flesh in the nether regions.

What goes meow-meow on the roof tiles? - Τι κάνει νιάου-νιάου στα κεραμίδια; (Ti kanei niaou-niaou sta keramidia?)

Meaning: the answer is obvious

What meows on the rooftops is, of course, a cat, so the question has an obvious answer. The phrase is used in rhetorical questions to refer to something self-evident but unstated. Greek cats, incidentally, don't say *meow* but *niaou*, a pronunciation difference that only a cat could explain.

What tobacco one smokes - Τι καπνό φουμάρει (Ti kapno foumarei)

Meaning: what kind of character one is; what one believes or is up to

For years rural men, especially in Macedonia and western Greece where tobacco is farmed, prided themselves on being able to smoke the rawest, heaviest tobacco they could get their hands on as an indication of manliness. Those who preferred the milder, packaged cigarettes were despised as city wimps.

Interesting is the use of the verb *foumaro* to denote smoking. An obvious derivative of the Italian *fumare,* and rarely used now, it indicates the probable introduction of tobacco to Greece by Italian traders in the 16th century.

Another proffered explanation is that the amount of smoke emerging from a house signified its degree of prosperity, ie the householder could afford enough fuel to keep the house warm and his family fed, hence a sign of status.

Where you hear of many cherries, carry a small basket - Όπου ακούς πολλά κεράσια, κράτα μικρό καλάθι (Opou akous polla kerasia, krata mikro kalathi)

Meaning: Don't believe big promises

Another expression from the frugal and realist rural environment. Greece has never been a country where food has grown in especial abundance, so reports of such abundance are naturally to be taken with a grain of salt, to be seen before being believed.

In psychological terms, it could be argued that a spare agricultural economy could overcompensate by encouraging the trait of talkativeness and boasting, both salient in the Greek character.

Weather and nature

A hole in the water - Μια τρύπα στο νερό (Mia trypa sto nero)
Meaning: futility; a useless exercise
One of the most futile actions one can do is try to make a hole in water. As such it has become a metaphor for something impossible to carry out. It also has come to mean the result of well-meaning efforts that ultimately come to nought.

Beaten air - Αέρας κοπανιστός (Aeras kopanistos)
Meaning: nonsense; hot air
The verb employed here is that associated with the preparation of food, such as beating and crushing grain to make flour – that is, refining. Refined air, then, is next to nothing.

Becoming smoke - Γίνομαι καπνός (Yinomai kapnos)
Meaning: disappearing; getting out of here
This is used to refer to someone who runs away or hides out of fear or embarrassment. Probably faster than actual smoke dissolves in the air.

Casting a black stone - Ρίχνω μαύρη πέτρα (Rihno mavri petra)
Meaning: good riddance; having nothing more to do with something
To the Greeks and other Mediterranean peoples, black is the colour of seriousness, which is partly why so much fashion is bound up with this colour. When someone quits a job in anger, moves out of an inhospitable environment or leaves one's abusive spouse, such a person figuratively (in the villages of old

it was done literally) casts a black stone behind to indicate the seriousness and irrevocableness of the decision.

Don't drip, don't rain - Μη στάξει μη βρέξει (Mi staxei mi vrexei)

Meaning: delicate, fragile, needing protection

In the days before antibiotics and other effective medicines, colds, flu and pneumonia carried off many people. It was thus imperative to keep risk-prone individuals such as sickly children out of the rain. From there the phrase was expanded to take in the sense of protection in general, including valuable and fragile objects. (See **Like the iris of the eye**, p 31)

Eating wood - Τρώω ξύλο (Troo xylo)

Meaning: taking a beating, being physically attacked

Beating with a stick or cane, either for punishment or out of malice, was once far more common than it is today. Hence the term "wood" has come to denote any form of blow, slap or even kick delivered with hostile intent.

Worthy of note is the victim mentality inherent in the wording. This ties in with the Greeks' curious historical perception of themselves as the eternal victims of alien forces. The perpetrator's usage would be "to load with wood" *(xylofortono)*. This form, though, is less common.

Falling cloud - Πέφτει σύννεφο (Peftei synnefo)

Meaning: coming down in abundance

Rain is essentially a falling cloud. Thus the reference here is to something raining down, such as angry words or blows. A typical extension is **wood falling like a cloud** (το ξύλο πέφτει σύννεφο) *(to xylo peftei synnefo)*, meaning a rain of blows on someone. (See **Eating wood**, p 56).

Falling from the clouds - Πέφτω απ'τα σύννεφα (Pefto ap'ta synnefa)

Meaning: being astonished; coming down to earth with a bump

The sense here is of one being unpleasantly surprised by what one had previously idealised. It would be nice to think that the phrase was inspired by Aristophanes' comedy *The Clouds*, which portrayed the philosopher as a sky-dwelling dreamer.

Forty waves - Σαράντα κύματα (Saranda kymata)
Meaning: into the wilderness; of unknown fate
The number forty has always had a symbolic importance in Greece as a symbol for many. This derives probably from the forty-day fasting and mourning periods decreed by the Orthodox Church. Forty waves, by this explanation, stands for the high seas and, by extension, for any figurative uncontrolled situation in which one's fate is uncertain.

Going with the waters - Πηγαίνω με τα νερά (Pigaino me ta nera)
Meaning: going along or agreeing with someone
This phrase sounds like it originated in the islands, which until the 20th century were self-contained communities. Each port had its own "waters", so entering that port would mean having to be on one's good behaviour.
The expression is now used as diplomatic advice to someone not to cross or antagonise someone else seen as potentially harmful or dangerous.

Having one's nest soiled - Έχω τη φωλιά μου λερωμένη (Eho ti folia mou leromeni)
Meaning: Having something to hide, a skeleton in the cupboard, the pot calling the kettle black
The spirit here is essentially that of being sinful oneself, hence unqualified to cast the first stone. A bird that soils it own nest can hardly be in a position to insist on the cleanliness of other nests. The phrase most often pops up in political issues, whose protagonists make a career of soiling all manner of nests.

It's raining over there - Πέρα βρέχει (Pera vrehei)
Meaning: not having a clue; not knowing what's going on
Here's another one that is semantically hard to crack. Very likely the image is of someone absent-minded, gazing at the rain in the distance while ignoring more pressing matters closer to hand.

Like the snows - Σαν τα χιόνια (San ta hionia)

Meaning: long time no see

Originating probably in the islands or southern Greece, where snow is infrequent, it's an interesting example of a style of imagery going back to Homer. The phrase paints a common human sentiment in the colours of nature.

Besides the vividness of the analogy, there is a subtext revealing the Greeks' social proclivities. Seeing someone again after a long time is an overtly emotional experience for the Greeks, hence the urge to deck it in colourful figurative terms. Snow, moreover, in the Greek islands is enough of a rarity to be welcomed rather than feared when it arrives.

Luck a mountain - Τύχη Βουνό (Tyhi vouno)

Meaning: extraordinary good luck; deliverance from certain death or injury

The mountain (see **Mountains are used to the snows,** p 58) was the traditional metaphor for sheer size. Unfortunately, the modern Greek media have degraded it into the weariest of overused cliches. No news involving the passengers of some train, plane, ship or motor vehicle escaping misfortune is free of this expression.

Making a sea of something - Τα κάνω θάλασσα (Ta kano thalassa)

Meaning: making a mess

The image of the unstructured and unpredictable sea is here used to stand for disintegration, as in an angry sea washing away solid structures. As in all figurative speech involving the sea, this one very likely originated in or around the Aegean.

Mountains are used to the snows - Συνηθισμένα τα Βουνά απ'τα χιόνια (Synithismena ta vouna ap'ta hionia)

Meaning: an experienced person does not fear adversity

The use here of the mountain metaphor, common to northern and central Greece and the Peloponnese, denotes not only physical toughness but also strength of character.

Of the string and the pole - Του σκοινιού και του παλουκιού (Tou skiniou kai tou paloukiou)

Meaning: rudimentary; rough and ready; bad quality person

Things assembled with string and poles, such as a rudimentary fishing rod and line, tend to be ineffectual. Also, string and pole could refer to hanging, a common fate in olden times of poor-quality people.

Seeing a white day - Βλέπω άσπρη μέρα (Vlepo aspri mera)

Meaning: getting rid of problems at last; seeing prosperity

To the Greeks, the colours black and white are laden with emotional associations. Black is equivalent to death and negativity (see **Casting a black stone,** p 55). White, as a consequence, is the warder-off of those dire things, and thus preferable for such basic pursuits as painting boats and houses. A white day is thus a day – awaited perhaps for years or decades – when money and other worries will cease and life can be celebrated in its fullness. Incidentally, no ethics are attached to how one might achieve this desired state of affairs.

Speaking of winds and waters - Μιλάω περί ανέμων και υδάτων (Milao peri anemon kai ydaton)

Meaning: small talk, inconsequential chatter

Wind and water are metonyms for the weather in general. Curiously enough, the phrase is couched in archaic purist Greek, which emphasises the artificiality of the supposed talk. In modern usage it connotes a situation in which small talk (ie about the weather) is an attempt to evade more serious issues for discussion.

The river taking it - Το παίρνει το ποτάμι (To pairnei to potami)

Meaning: going to waste; a futile loss

Rivers in Greece are generally benign in the summer. In the winter, though, they can become raging torrents, threatening man and beast. Something washed away by such a river would be truly gone for good. There could also be an echo of Ancient Greek purification rites here.

The sky coming a distaff - Έρχεται ο ουρανός σφοντύλι (Erhetai o ouranos sfondyli)
>Meaning: out of the blue; a blow where it's least expected
>An analysis of this expression sets its origin in pre-industrial days when the average woman's time was taken up in large part with spinning wool on her distaff. It was not uncommon, when the husband was away in the fields, for the occasional prettier wife to be chatted up by some local lothario, who would receive the distaff on his head (out of the "sky") for his pains. (See **Taking it on the skull,** p 36)

The wild come to drive away the tame - Ήρθαν τ' άγρια να διώξουν τα ήμερα (Irthan t'agria na dioxoun ta imera)
>Meaning: taking over something by force; usurping
>In the wilder regions of Greece livestock were (and still are) at the mercy of predators such as wolves and hawks. The image of the wolf entering the pen to scatter the sheep has come to illustrate domestic or workplace instances where a comfortable situation is overturned by an uncouth newcomer.

The windmill happens - Γίνεται μύλος (Yinetai mylos)
>Meaning: chaos, disorder.
>Windmills used to be the prime means of making flour in the Aegean islands. The grinding of grain to powder may account for the image of general disintegration. Or perhaps the incessant turning of the mill sails in the wind suggests a sense of perpetual and ultimately meaningless motion.

Life experiences

And to yours - Και στα δικά σου (Kai sta dika sou)
>Meaning: may you, too, get married
>Some phrases in every language have assumed such ritual

importance that not to utter them in the strictly defined environment would be almost unthinkable. This phrase is one of these. It is used at one event only, a wedding, and at a specific time – after the ceremony is over.

That's when the guests are chatting away in the church courtyard, waiting for the newlyweds to emerge and clutching their little bags of mandatory sugared almonds (a fertility totem). Then every unmarried person under the age of 40 or so has to endure a veritable barrage of "and to yours" (meaning nuptials). This overt social pressure to get married – a relic of the days when Greece was underpopulated and family cohesion was the only real security – still works.

And you'll sing a song - Και θα πεις κι ένα τραγούδι (Kai tha peis ki ena tragoudi)

Meaning: you'll do it and like it

A good, old-fashioned formula for parental compulsion. It seems to have originated in primary schools, where lessons were made more palatable by singsong sessions, including the regulation singing of the national anthem in front of the flag in the morning.

At the five roads - Στους πέντε δρόμους (Stous pende dromous)

Meaning: homeless, destitute, unemployed

The crossroads image as a symbol of not knowing where to go or what to do is here evident, though why it should consist of five rather than four roads is vague. The number five is probably a memory of a typical Greek small town, which must not have had more than half a dozen principal thoroughfares.

At the good sittings - Στα καλά καθούμενα (Sta kala kathoumena)

Meaning: unexpectedly; out of the blue

The image is that of someone happily sitting, minding one's own business, when disturbed by a sudden and unwelcome event. It also refers to an act by someone that is out of character and hence inexplicable.

At the light and put out - Στο άψε σβήσε (Sto apse svise)
Meaning: in short order; in a jiffy
The awkward literal English translation utterly fails to capture the flavour of this pithy expression. It may be a carryover from the times when a home fire might easily go out if not constantly tended. Or it could have come from the image of a match being lighted and then quickly blown out after serving its purpose.

At the P and F - Στο πι και φι (Sto pi kai fi)
Meaning: promptly, right away
This expression has been around for many decades, yet it remains hard to figure out. The best the author can offer is that the Greek letters P and F (*pi* and *fi,* or *phi*), are those on fire systems outlets. They stand for *(Pyrosvestiki Folia).* Such equipment, when needed, is of course used without delay.

Black hour - Μαύρη ώρα (Mavri ora)
Meaning: an unfortunate or regrettable time
The colour black among the Greeks has a vividly symbolic importance as the ultimate negative quality. Someone will often be heard lamenting, for example, that it was a "black hour" in which a certain lover was met for the first time, or an unlucky business decision taken.
Psychologically, it reveals a penchant for blaming vague outside powers for one's own mistakes – a typically Greek trait.

Blowing on it, and it not getting cold - Το φυσάω και δεν κρυώνει (To fisao kai den kryonei)
Meaning: nursing a grudge; burning with revenge
When one is slighted or suffers an injustice, the mental sensation can be likened to heat. As a hot food or beverage burns the tongue, so injustice burns the mind. Yet unlike food or drink, a sense of being wronged doesn't cool down when blown on. Rather the opposite, in fact, like fanning flames.

Careful the chandelier - Σιγά τον πολυέλαιο (Siga ton polyelaio)

Meaning: big deal; don't make such a fuss; don't put on airs

Chandeliers in Greece were once the exclusive possessions of the wealthy and their imitators. Hence their symbolising false luxury and a certain fragility in the popular mind. Therefore if someone boasts of some personal achievement or possession and puts on airs while doing it, the sarcastic reply "careful [or don't break] the chandelier" is usually enough to deflate the boaster.

The phrase most probably has a practical origin in house-moving or home repair. Large and cumbersome objects such as ladders and furniture have to be handled carefully so as not to smash any valuable chandeliers that might be hanging from the ceiling. (See also **Careful the eggs**, p 41)

Cloth with cloth - Πανί με πανί (Pani me pani)

Meaning: broke, penniless

When the cloth sides of one's pockets come together, with nothing between them, then there's nothing in the pocket.

Coming out of one's clothes - Βγαίνω από τα ρούχα μου (Vgaino ap'ta rouha mou)

Meaning: becoming angry or indignant

There seems to be an echo here of the Biblical rending of the mantle in cases of great emotional stress. Certainly, when one is abnormally angry it can seem that the very clothes one wears are too confining.

Cradle that rocked you - Κούνια που σε κούναγε (Kounia pou se kounage)

Meaning: you must be mad; there must be something wrong with you

It was once believed that abrupt shaking during infancy – such as a particularly violent rock of the cradle — could addle the child's brain and result in an abnormal adult. Thus if someone comes out with erratic or unpopular opinions, one might say that as a baby his or her cradle was given a particularly hard lurch. The phrase is almost always used in the second person, as a direct address, and in a contemptuous tone. (See **Sleep on that side,** p 73)

Cry for them, Haralambos Κλάψ'τα, Χαράλαμπε (Klaps'ta Haralambe)

Meaning: it's a disaster; forget it

No one seems to know who this Kharalambos was. One tradition has it that he was an Athenian civil servant who found himself out of a job after a change of government. Even today, a party that wins a national election sacks as many civil servants of the previous party as it dares, and replaces them with its own voters.

Those thus sacked in the late 19th and early 20th centuries would gather at the cafes in central Klafthmonos Square (literally, the Square of Weeping) to bewail their fate. The "them" in the phrase indicates life's conditions, bleak to someone out of work.

Cutting movement - Κόβω κίνηση (Kovo kinisi)

Meaning: keeping a lookout; monitoring a situation

This is almost certainly a linguistic fruit of the city underworld, for two reasons.

First, it well describes the act of checking the comings and goings of people for a distinct purpose. Second, it employs the verb to cut, which associates the mind with the knife, the chief weapon of the petty-criminal class. These days the phrase is used in any situation requiring increased vigilance for whatever reason.

Eating the place - Τρώω τον τόπο (Troo ton topo)

Meaning: searching high and low

The verb to eat in Greek (see **Eating someone,** p 43) is employed also to mean getting the better of someone or eliminating a threat. A search for something lost, then, is likened to "eliminating" the places where the lost object or missing person could possibly be.

Economising them - Τα οικονομάω (Ta ikonomao)

Meaning: making money; enjoying profits

The verb to economise in Greek is the polar opposite of its English meaning of to save and be frugal. The Greeks have never been afflicted with the wealth guilt complex, and one who "economises" – that is, makes money by fair means or foul – is a role model to be admired. The phrase carries a taste of Odyssean cunning employed in the process of enrichment.

Emptying the corner - Αδειάζω τη γωνιά (Adeiazo ti gonia)

Meaning: leaving; making oneself scarce

This could be an echo of the time when most Greek rural homes were small, with precious little living space. To empty a corner would mean to leave the house. In these more affluent days, the phrase is used most often in the imperative, to tell someone to get lost.

Everything is paid for here - Όλα εδώ πληρώνονται (Ola edo plironontai)

Meaning: justice will be rendered in this life

This is another durable piece of paganism that has survived to become part of modern Greek thought. The Greeks don't quite trust the Christian doctrine that ultimate justice will be found only in the next world. They harbour a conviction that evildoers somehow will get their just deserts before they die – a belief so strongly at variance with reality that one wonders at its longevity.

Falling dry - Πέφτω ξερός (Pefto xeros)

Meaning: dropping dead; being astonished

The word *xeros* means dry in the sense of barren or organically withered. Someone dying suddenly, from whatever cause, can be said to have become a barren organism. In a lighter vein, the phrase is also used to convey stupefaction or sudden astonishment.

Falling in shallow water - Πέφτω στα ρηχά (Pefto sta riha)

Meaning: getting off lightly

If one were to fall into a body of water, after some act of rash misjudgement, to land in shallow rather than deep water would be fortunate. The image is now used to describe all instances of getting off lightly. A variation is **falling on the softs** (πέφτω στα μαλακά) *(pefto sta malaka)*.

Finding the end - Βρίσκω την άκρη (Vrisko tin akri)
Meaning: solving a problem; finding the cause

The Greek word *akri* is usually translatable as the end of, say, a rope or stick, or the edge of a table or building, or the tip of a tail. There's an echo here of Alexander the Great's radical solution to the problem of the Gordian knot that no one before him had been able to unravel – or "find the end" of the string. As all who have grappled with intractable knots will attest, finding the end of the string is halfway to untying them.

Finding them poles - Τα βρίσκω παλούκια (Ta vrisko paloukia)
Meaning: encountering unexpected difficulty

The poles in this case could be either birching rods used by the teachers of old or the poles of a fence that would presumably deter someone from raiding a vegetable field. The expression in its present usage carries a certain connotation of encountering unexpected difficulties in a task previously thought to be easy.

Full stop and dash - Τελεία και παύλα (Teleia kai pavla)
Meaning: that's final; an end to the matter

In Greek schools and public services until recently, essays and reports were concluded with a dash after the final full stop, to indicate the end. The advent of the computer and word processing ended that practice.

Glass nails - Γυαλιά-καρφιά (Yalia karfia)
Meaning: destroyed, in pieces

The phrase is generally used to describe the result of some violence or accident on physical property. The image is that of broken glass and protruding nails.

Go to the good - Άει στο καλό! (Aei sto kalo!)

Meaning: go away; go to hell

The Greeks have a history of using propitiatory terms to ward off an imagined evil that could come from naming evil things. In ancient Greek tragedy, for example, the Furies – those satanic tormentors of the psyche – were also called the Eumenides, or Benevolent Ones. In short, something bad is termed good in order to propitiate the evil itself.

That said, however, all Greeks enthusiastically employ the real thing, ie **go to the devil** (άντε στο διάολο) *(ade sto diaolo)*, with the last word drawn out in a satisfying curse.

Good having of the things - Καλώς ερχόντων των πραγμάτων (Kalos erhonton ton pragmaton)

Meaning: assuming all is well

The blandness of the wording here may be a relic of the old belief, pagan as well as Christian, that to boldly state one's future plans is somehow to provoke the gods. It's the equivalent of the English "God willing", though in a secular society it has lost its original religious sense.

The cadence of the phrase carries a pleasing lilt, while the curious use of *erhonton,* an archaic participle no longer used in ordinary speech, gives it a slightly pompous air.

Good road - Καλό δρόμο (Kalo dromo)

Meaning: safe journey; Godspeed

Land travel in old Greece was never very secure, with the constant threat of brigands, wild animals and other menaces. Therefore the wish expressed here had a very real purpose. Yet even today, with modern Greece's road accident rate among the highest in Europe, it's a good idea to have this sentiment at one's back before taking the wheel.

Hold on to your clothes to have half - Κράτα τα ρούχα σου για να 'χεις τα μισά (Krata ta rouha sou ya na 'heis ta misa)

Meaning: you can never be too careful

Such was the periodic insecurity of Greek society for centuries that literally nothing could be considered safe – not even one's clothes. Clothes here are a metonym for possessions in general, as they were literally the only possessions of many poor people. And, as the phrase shows, they could not really even be sure of those.

In a good place - Σε καλή μεριά (Se kali meria)
Meaning: may your new money or acquisition remain safe

This phrase has become a trite ritual addressed to someone who has had a sudden stroke of good fortune such as winning the lottery or getting a big raise in pay. Literally it's a wish (as often as not masking envy) that wherever the money is stashed it will be safe from thieves or in a safe investment.

In one's blacks - Στις μαύρες μου (Stis mavres mou)
Meaning: in depression

The use of the colour black to indicate depression cuts across many languages and cultures. In the Greek case what stands out is the plural usage of "blacks". Here could be a hint of the old belief in evil spirits (such as the Furies of ancient tradition) that were highly adept at playing brutal mind games with people.

It's being played - Παίζεται (Paizetai)
Meaning: the outcome is still uncertain; a decision has yet to be made

Almost certainly this image derives from football matches, whose outcome is uncertain until the final whistle. The ball, being played, can enter the goal on either side. Thus in the mind of someone who still hasn't decided about something, the ball in their minds is still being "played".

It's not play-laugh - Δεν είναι παίξε-γέλασε (Den einai paixe-yelase)
Meaning: take this seriously; it's no fun and games

The phrase "play-laugh" in Greek suggests doing something for fun and laughing about it afterwards. It's addressed to anyone who has a flighty, irresponsible attitude to a certain task or life itself.

It's the ninth of the month - Εννέα έχει ο μήνας (Ennea ehei o minas)
Meaning: unaware, indifferent; spaced out

Here's a difficult one to trace. Not knowing that it's a certain date of the month would indicate a degree of unawareness or stupidity, though believing that every day is the ninth would betray a drastically more serious mental condition.

A more socio-economic explanation is that Greek civil servants used to be paid every ninth of the month. Thus that date came to signify a carefree attitude (at least for a few days).

Joy to the thing! - Χαρά στο πράμα! (Hara sto prama!)
Meaning: so what?

The sarcasm in the phrase is obvious. It almost always betrays a certain envy when someone else enjoys good fortune or boasts about some achievement or possession. (See **Careful the chandelier,** p 63)

Knowing where the four go - Ξέρω πού παν τα τέσσερα (Xero pou pan'ta tessera)
Meaning: being aware; knowing the ropes

The number four has always had a certain significance in Greek lore (see **Forty waves** and **Having them 400,** pp 57, 16). Here it could merely reflect the basic importance of the two hands and two feet, whose coordination is necessary for a great many tasks. Someone, thus, who "doesn't know where the four go" can be considered quite incompetent.

Life to you - Ζωή σε σένα (Zoi se sena)
Meaning: condolences

The affirmation of life in the face of death is the ultimate purpose of this strictly ritualised phrase, said to someone who has just suffered the loss of a parent or other close family member. The propitiatory wish is that death stop at that member and allow the others to go on living.

Lifting - Σηκώνω (Sikono)

Meaning: tolerating, standing for

The notion of toleration as a physical burden is an echo of the eons when most people survived by hard physical labour, and under despotic rule at that. Thus one commonly hears a Greek declaiming that he or she will not "lift" certain words or behaviour from another.

Light lantern - Φως φανάρι (Fos fanari)

Meaning: obvious; as clear as day

This phrase is a good example of the old literary practice, common in the Bible and in oriental writings, of augmented repetition for emphasis. It's not enough for something to be clear as light; it has to be as specifically clear and focused as a lantern.

My old craft a sieve - Παλιά μου τέχνη κόσκινο (Palia mou tehni koskino)

Meaning: getting up to one's old habits or tricks

In Greek the same word, *tekhni,* is used for art and craft. There's a popular cynical proverb to the effect that one is wise to learn a trade while young, then abandon it in favour of doing things that *really* make money. If at some point one falls on hard times and goes hungry, then is the time to take up the honest trade again. The sieve indicates that in the meantime one's skills might have acquired a few holes.

Not burning a nail - Δεν μου καίγεται καρφί (Den mou kaiyetai karfi)

Meaning: not caring; not giving a damn

The Greeks employ the verb to burn for non-combustive meanings as well, including that of wasting or using up. In carpentry, wasting a nail is of no huge consequence, therefore not worth worrying about.

Not putting it down - Δεν το βάζω κάτω (Den to vazo kato)

Meaning: not giving up; persisting

This is an image from warfare. To admit defeat is to lay down one's arms. From the combat sphere the phrase has been eagerly adopted into civilian life to use in any situation where persistence and stubbornness are seen as necessary, especially in cases of righting an injustice.

Not wanting to see it drawn - Δεν θέλω να το δω ούτε ζωγραφιστό (De thelo na to do oute zografisto)

Meaning: wanting nothing whatever to do with something or someone

When one despises something or someone, one naturally does not even wish to see a picture of the thing or person so despised. The phrase appears to have originated in the pre-photography era in its reference to drawn images.

Incidentally, the Greeks tend to use the same verb for to draw and to paint, *zografizo*. This indicates the relative lack of popularity of the visual arts which can be traced to the Byzantine era's rejection of Renaissance realistic art, and which lingers today.

Of the getting on - Της προκοπής (Tis prokopis)

Meaning: worth something; of good quality

The Greek word *prokopi* is one of those larded with connotations that are more important than their literal meaning. Generally translatable as progress, or "getting on" in life, it has a heavy flavour of self-improvement and work ethic.

This points to an origin in rural Greece, which has traditionally valued hard work and bettering oneself, in contrast to the Athenian and Asia Minor habits of spending the day in idle political talk and coffee consumption.

One joy - Μια χαρά (Mia hara)

Meaning: all right, in good order, no problem

When things are progressing smoothly and according to plan, or when someone feels well and is free of illness, the phrase springs automatically to Greek lips. A more cynical version indicates the precise opposite: **one joy and two terrors** (μια χαρά και δυο τρομάρες) *(mia hara kai dyo tromares)*; that is, whatever is all right has been overshadowed by twice as much that is wrong.

One's life a bicycle - Η ζωή μου ποδήλατο (I zoi mou podilato)

Meaning: being given a hard time; going through a rough phase

The origin of this curious expression is hard to assess. Greece, as a mountainous country, has never been amenable to cycling. Then again, it reflects perhaps the act of learning to ride a bicycle, with its wobblings and spills.

It could also be a facile spinoff from the older **one's life black** (Η ζωή μου μαύρη) *(I zoi mou mavri)*, whose drift is rather more obvious, if a tad dramatic.

Out-heart - Έξω καρδιά (Exo kardia)

Meaning: jolly, generous, uncaring of the morrow

Being "out-heart" is one of the Greeks' most prized personality traits, though honoured as much in the breach as in the observance. The term conjures up images of winebibbing and syrtaki-dancing till all hours, with a contemptuous disregard of the finances involved.

Psychosomatically, the phrase gives one a mental relief of sorts, as it seems (in Greek) to open up the heart, freeing it from uptight preoccupations and worldly cares. There could even be some connection with the Greeks' longevity here.

Raising the place - Σηκώνω τον τόπο (Sikono ton topo)

Meaning: making a great fuss

The verb *sikono* also means getting someone out of bed. Any ruckus made at night – common in a land of warm summer nights – would therefore disturb the sleep of a number of people.

Round-sitting - Στρογγυλοκάθομαι (Srongylokathomai)

Meaning: sitting comfortably

The actual image conveyed here, vivid and very specific, is of someone plumping themselves down onto a chair or settee in a conspicuous display of indolence. The "round" could possibly refer to the large buttocks involved in the sitting down. The definite sarcastic tone of the phrase suggests that it originated among the less well-off, to whom the luxury-loving upper classes were objects of contempt.

Run and seek - Τρέχα-γύρευε (Treha yireve)
Meaning: forget it; there's no point
The image here is of someone running about in a futile quest to get something done – an apt portrait, for example, of the tribulations attendant on the notorious Greek bureaucracy. Indeed, this could well be the origin of the expression, as even today a good many of the people hurrying around central Athens on any given weekday morning are in hot pursuit of red tape requirements for almost every constructive activity in life.

Shaking them - Τα τινάζω (Ta tinazo)
Meaning: dying
Most languages employ expressions that attempt to make light of the grimness of death, and this is one of them. However, though uttered in an irreverent manner, the image most likely derives from the convulsions - or "shaking" of the limbs - that sometimes accompany death throes.
The verb *tinazo*, though, also means to blow up. Here death can be viewed, as it were, as a blowing up, or destruction, of life.

Sleeping the good time - Κοιμάμαι του καλού καιρού (Kimamai tou kalou kairou)
Meaning: sleeping soundly; being a slug-a-bed
In a hardworking rural society sleep has always been a luxury. Therefore only those enjoying "the good time" – that is, prosperity – could afford to sleep a lot. The slightly censorious tone attached to the original meaning has remained.

Sleep on that side - Απ'αυτό το πλευρό να κοιμάσαι (Ap'afto to plevro na kimasai)
Meaning: if that's what you think, you must be crazy
It was once believed that sleeping on one's left side was somehow bad for the heart and hence the brain. Therefore

someone insisting on an unpopular view, or clearly in the wrong in a discussion, will be told that sleeping "on that side" is what causes him or her to be so off track.

Small the bad - Μικρό το κακό (Mikro to kako)

Meaning: not much damage done

It's not too difficult to decipher the meaning from the wording here. The main interest lies in its being an excellent example of Greek semantic structuring. Unlike, for example, English, whose meanings rely almost entirely on word order, in Greek (and Latin) the opposite is true. Phrasal elements can be arranged any old way as long as the grammatical inflections and conjugations are maintained. "Small the bad", in that word order, makes no sense in English, but in Greek it's perfectly clear, as it would also be with the words changed around. The tradition goes back to Archilochos, a 7th century BC poet who was the unrivalled master of such phrase-condensation.

Something's running - Κάτι τρέχει (Kati trehei)

Meaning: something's going on

Greek is very free with the use of the verb to run to describe processes of any kind. For example, time, taximeters and expenses "run" incessantly. The phrase could be a contraction of **something's running in the Gipsy quarter** (Κάτι τρέχει στα γύφτικα) *(Kati trehei sta yiftika),* meaning "no big deal", which shines some light on the marginal social status that Greece's Gipsy communities have even today. They still tend to be somewhat noisier and more chaotic – and maybe more dangerous – places than the bourgeois majority, hence to be looked down on.

The instruments begin - Αρχίζουν τα όργανα (Arhizoun ta organa)

Meaning: the argument starts

Since one of the most popular pastimes in Greece, it seems, is disputing in a loud voice, it may sound to some as music to their ears, hence the analogy with musical instruments. Or, as some say, when the patrons of a taverna got into a fight, the band was told to start playing to cover up the noise.

Touch red - Πιάσε κόκκινο (Piase kokkino)

Meaning: cross your fingers

As the traditional colour of joy in Greece, red is also the colour of hope and good tidings. Descended as it is from the idea of the redeeming blood of Christ, red dominates Orthodox Easter in the form of the ubiquitous red-dyed eggs. To touch red, then, is to hope that things will turn out well. Communists, naturally, tend to favour the phrase, though from a radically different ideological viewpoint.

Unbutton yourself - Ξεκουμπίσου (Xekoumbisou)

Meaning: get out; leave now

This is a difficult one to trace. Perhaps the only feasible explanation (admittedly a stab in the dark) is that at one time it was the habit of impecunious men to walk into clothes shops and keep trying on clothes until ordered out by the shopkeeper. They would thus have to unbutton themselves, ie doff the apparel, and leave in a hurry.

Then again, someone summarily sacked from a factory or shop would surely be required to "unbutton" the overall or other working apparel before leaving.

Who to your grace? - Ποιος στη χάρη σου (Pios sti khari sou)

Meaning: aren't you lucky?

The grace meant here is that which descends on one who comes into some unexpected good fortune. As a way of flattering the one thus favoured, it's conventional to ask the question of who else can be counted so lucky. Cynics, though, would say there is more than a trace of envy in the expression.

Working one - Σε δουλεύω (Se doulevo)

Meaning: deceiving someone; taking the mickey

There is a suggestion here of "working [someone] over" for fun. The most common specific variant is **Are you working me?** (Με δουλεύεις;) *(Me douleveis?)* meaning "are you kidding me?" This can also take on hostile overtones, as in a road argument, for example.

Another common variant is **working one with a fine stitch** (Δουλεύω με ψιλό γαζί) *(Doulevo me psilo gazi),* meaning a particularly blatant form of deception.

Historical memories

Becoming an ancient Greek - Γίνομαι αρχαίος (Yinomai arhaios)

Meaning: freezing in the cold

This is probably a late 1970s city invention. In the classic Greek tendency to pictorial hyperbole, shivering in the cold is likened to being as stiff as a statue; that is, as the statues that are all that's left these days of the ancient Greeks.

Being an Englishman - Είμαι Άγγλος (Eimai Anglos)

Meaning: being punctual

In the long and tortured love-hate relationship which the Greeks have always had with the English, the one thing besides football that the Greeks have envied in the English is their unfailing punctuality. To this day, the English in Greece invariably impress the locals with this quality, which to the average Greek – to whom time is an extremely flexible concept – is admirable, if a tad naive.

Bursting it - Το σκάω (To skao)

Meaning: getting out of here; fleeing, escaping

This vivid metaphor most likely arose out of the Greek Independence War of 1821-29. The Greek verb to burst is also the vernacular for to explode. Bands of irregulars would sneak up to Turkish outposts or ships, mostly at night, place the explosives and flee.

There is also a faint association with the imperative **burst!** *(skase!),* meaning "shut up!" As the average Greek is a naturally voluble person, blocking the flow of speech could conceivably trigger some sort of explosion.

Changing one's lights - Μου αλλάζει τα φώτα (Mou allazei ta fota)

Meaning: undergoing or making someone undergo an ordeal; getting revenge on someone

This almost certainly goes back to the time of Ottoman rule (mid-15th to early 19th century), when forced conversions to Islam were a periodic occurrence. Beatings and other forms of torture were sometimes used to this end, hence the changing of the victim's "lights" or religious faith.

For fear of the Jews - Για τον φόβο των Ιουδαίων (Ya ton fovo ton Ioudaion)

Meaning: for fear of social ostracism

The phrase is from John 7:13 in the *New Testament*, which tells how many people in Judaea were afraid to talk about Jesus "for fear of the Jews". Scarcely surprisingly, the Orthodox Church popularised it, giving free rein to an anti-Semitism that still lingers in some church circles.

From where one's cap holds - Από πού κρατάει η σκούφια (Apo pou krataei i skoufia)

Meaning: where one is from; one's identity or belief

In the 19th century, when Greece was still a multicultural society, a person's ethnic or religious identity could be easily seen from the headgear. A Turk, for example, would be wearing a fez, a Jew a yarmulke, a Western European a top hat, an Albanian a round *skoufo* (or *skoufia*) and so on. The verb to hold in the case is equivalent to the English to hail [from].

Grabbing the pope by the balls - Πιάνω τον Πάπα απ'τ' αρχίδια (Piano ton Papa ap'ta arkhidia)

Meaning: boasting of some achievement or distinction

Throughout the ages, the Orthodox Greeks' attitude to the popes in Rome, and the Catholic Church in general, has varied from distrust to open hostility. In more recent times this animosity has faded, yet the phrase lives on triumphantly. In Greek thinking, to manage to approach the pope close enough to seize him by his privates would be the apotheosis of heroic achievement. The phrase is used, however, in a sarcastic sense to describe someone's megalomaniac boasting.

Not a fly on one's sword - Ούτε μύγα στο σπαθί μου (Oute miga sto spathi mou)

Meaning: having one's honour intact; rejecting criticism

Greek swordsmanship goes back to the Independence War, an epochal event that has defined the modern national narrative in many ways. The warrior image has since been revived and re-incorporated into the manhood discourse. The sword is subconsciously a phallic symbol, representing manliness and virtue. Keeping one's sword (ie honour) shiny, not even allowing a fly to alight on it, is to symbolically preserve one's manhood. (See **Not a flea on the back of your neck**, p 48)

The suitcase goes a long way - Πάει μακρυά η βαλίτσα (Paei makrya i valitza)

Meaning: there's more to this than meets the eye; it's a long story

This could be an echo of the time in the late 19th and most of the 20th centuries when masses of poor Greeks emigrated to North America, Australia and Germany. Their rickety string-bound luggage carried their worldly possessions truly a long way.

To those left behind, who probably would never see their loved ones again, the image of the suitcase would be a powerfully emotional one. The phrase also carries a connotation of "don't get into it; the truth lies where you don't expect it."

With no government - Με καμμία κυβέρνηση (Me kammia kyvernisi)

Meaning: in no circumstances; no way

Modern Greece's frequent change of governments has left its mark in the popular parlance. Through most of the 19th and 20th centuries, when governments changed (often by coups and violence), what was expected of citizens could also change. Thus what was standard practice under one government might not be under the next.

What stands out here is the semantic equation of government

with circumstances in general, illustrating the importance that governments of all types have had for the daily lives of the politically-aware Greeks.

The otherworld

A tombstone on the soul - Ψυχοπλάκωμα (Psyhoplakoma)
Meaning: depressive anxiety
The Greeks' shuddery fascination with death emerges here in the image of someone with a gravestone pressing on the breast. Not the most comfortable of situations, but then again, depression rarely is.

At the bottom-bottom of the writing - Στο κάτω-κάτω της γραφής (Sto kato-kato tis grafis)
Meaning: in the final analysis
The word "writing", here rendered as *grafi,* also refers to the *Holy Scriptures*. Very likely the phrase is an echo of learned and sacerdotal disputes over the meaning of a particular passage of scripture. The term "bottom-bottom" means the real, underlying, hence true meaning. The phrase has come to stand for anything arrived at through logic and common sense.

Being a tomb - Είμαι τάφος (Eimai tafos)
Meaning: staying silent; keeping a secret
As the tomb is the quietest and most solemn of places, the Greeks' tendency to dramatise many of their idiolects is apparent here.

Don't even tell the priest - Μην το πεις ούτε του παπά (Min to peis oute tou papa)
Meaning: keep it entirely to yourself
Even in the days when it was common to confess oneself to a

priest, there were things that could not be said even to him, such as dark family or personal secrets. These were matters which, if revealed anywhere, would entail unbearable social shame. The phrase is used to encourage the keeping of deep, dark secrets.

Even the saint needs threatening - Και ο Άγιος φοβέρα θέλει (Kai o Agios fovera thelei)

Meaning: sometimes even a good deed must be accomplished by threats

This is the antithesis of **going cross in hand** (*qv*) as suggesting that being good and moral is all very well, but sometimes there's nothing like a bit of implied violence to get things moving. Both expressions are relics of Ottoman rule, when certain ideas inimical to true Christianity crept into the national psyche. Also, in the Greeks' own practical religious sense, not even a saint is necessarily free from the sins of timidity and procrastination.

God the assistant - Ο Θεός Βοηθός (O Theos voithos)

Meaning: only God can help us/you/one now

Unlike the solemn and dramatic colouring that the expression assumes in its English rendering, the Greeks toss it off carelessly in a huge variety of situations.

The very informality of its use testifies to the Greeks' easygoing relationship with the divine, often startling to a strict Catholic or Protestant. God, Christ, the Virgin Mary and the saints are figures that can be talked to daily – even scolded – on the most intimate terms. The phrase also evokes the semi-pagan image of a friendly deity giving your pet project a helpful push, when all that is humanly possible has been done.

Having a saint - Έχω Άγιο (Eho Agio)

Meaning: being lucky in escaping death

Virtually the same as **luck a mountain** (*qv*) but with a spiritual element. It reflects the Christian belief that intervention by a particular saint can avert tragedy and save lives. Yet as in the abovementioned equivalent, the media in a materialist society have done the phrase to death as a wan cliche.

If you are Christians - Αν είστε Χριστιανοί (An eiste Hristiani)

Meaning: if you are human, have any feelings at all

In times gone by, many people still took seriously the key Christian tenets of humility and compassion, which came to be idealised as the essence of being human. The phrase is uttered as a mild imprecation for those whose behaviour deviates conspicuously from the Christian ideal.

A related term, **my Christian** (Χριστιανέ μου) *(Hristiane mou)* is used as an exasperated form of address to someone who appears not to understand plain language, something a bit stronger than the English "my good fellow".

Joy of God - Χαρά Θεού (Hara Theou)

Meaning: pleasant, sunny weather

The Greeks have never failed to appreciate the generous amounts of sunshine with which their land has been blessed. The expression is mostly employed as subconscious thanks for those warm and balmy days in autumn, winter and spring, or when the sun comes out after a string of wet or cold days.

Like the devil incense - Σαν το διάολο το λιβάνι (San to diaolo to livani)

Meaning: avoiding like the plague

One of the original uses of incense in Orthodox Church services was to ward off evil spirits from the church and its congregation. It appears to have worked well, as the devil's frantic avoidance of incense has been total enough to create its own idiolect.

Like the unjust curse - Σαν την άδικη κατάρα (San tin adiki katara)

Meaning: wandering about with no rest

The dichotomy between an "unjust" and a supposedly "just" curse may seem curious, until one reflects on the pagan history of the Greeks. In this mindset, a "just" curse would settle on the head of its victim and that would be it. But an "unjust", or undeserved, curse would presumably fail to attach itself to its intended innocent victim and hence spend its time endlessly floating about.

Little angel - Αγγελούδι (Angeloudi)

Meaning: a child that suffers a tragic death or serious injury

Greek, like many tongues, is replete with usages that paraphrase death and its various manifestations in terms suggesting subconscious propitiation.

This can, in our era, give rise to grotesque concoctions, at which the sensationalist media are masters. Therefore today a television newsreader can say with a perfectly straight face that a child meeting a tragic end through accident, illness or crime has become "a little angel" in apparent symbolism of its innocence and undeserved fate. The Greek mindset recoils from describing children's fatal misfortunes in mere factual terms as too cold and unfeeling. Worth noting, though, is that such "angels" have a definite age limit, somewhere around twelve years old.

My faith came out upside down - Μου βγήκε η πίστη ανάποδα (Mou vgike i pisti anapoda)

Meaning: I worked till I dropped; the ordeal was almost too much

Here is a phrase with echoes of the old Christian-Muslim battlefield that Greece was for much of the 14th to the 19th centuries. With the Ottoman Turkish incursions that culminated in a 500-year subjugation, many Greeks were converted to Islam by force. This would take the form of physical torture, in which, more often than not, the victim was hung upside down until he or she recanted. (See **Changing one's lights, p 77**)

Not having one's God - Δεν έχω το θεό μου) (Den eho to theo mou)

Meaning: being wild and crazy; irreverent

The use of the deity here can come either capitalised or not, as in English. The ancient Greeks believed that the gods had definitely something to do with keeping people on the straight and narrow. In Christian times the notion was strengthened. In

Greek, the terms "the god" and "God" are the same, indicating the degree to which paganism and Christianity are mixed in the Greek mind.

The sense of the expression, however, does not change; someone lacking a god or God does not conform to the civilised rules of society, in either behaviour or speech.

To the devil's mother - Στου διαβόλου τη μάνα (Stou diavolou ti mana)

Meaning: a long way away; a place hard to find

Someone who has to travel a long way over a difficult route to a remote location will vent frustration by complaining that the destination is the very "devil's mother" to reach. A reasonable simile, since if the devil had a mother, she could be expected to reside as far away from human habitation as it is possible to get.

With cross in hand - Με το Σταυρό στο χέρι (Me to Stavro sto heri)

Meaning: going by the rules, being morally naive

Here is a phrase steeped in the unresolved conflicts which the Greeks have with the Christian faith two millennia after they embraced it.

To go "cross in hand", that is to follow the precepts of Christ and be morally upright, is something to be jeered at as naive. It may have something to do with the 400-year Ottoman Muslim rule which affected Greek culture more than most Greeks are willing to admit.

Thus there is a licence for larceny, including the right to take advantage of silly foreigners such as the Anglo-Saxons. Enough paganism remains in the national psyche to make acceptance of pure Christianity a problematic, though it's swept under the social carpet.

The expression appears to have originated with the Greeks of Asia Minor, who had to deal with Muslim authority, yet in turn brought Oriental attitudes to mainland Greece when they were expelled in the early 1920s. One cannot imagine the humble and devout peasantry of Greece proper being so dismissive of the cross.

With the soul in the mouth - Με την ψυχή στο στόμα (Me tin psyhi sto stoma)

Meaning: in fear and anxiety; with heart in mouth

This image emerges from the old belief that at death the soul exits through the mouth, along with the last breath. Extreme anxiety can reproduce such feelings of imminent demise. The expression is most often used when one is very late for something and after a great deal of hurry only just makes it, gasping (which may feel like one's soul is coming out).

The Greek Economy 1940-2004

By Mark Dragoumis

GREECE'S economic history reflects the slings and arrows of outrageous fortune that have bedevilled the country ever since it became independent in 1832. The road to development has been full of pitfalls such as coups, one fully fledged civil war, several Balkan wars, two World Wars, one devastating occupation, one global crisis, and two outright bankruptcies.

Mark Dragoumis has been observing Greek affairs both from inside the government and as a journalist since the 1940s. His informative and compelling account explains economic developments in the light of political ones.

Price: 9€

On sale at Eleftheroudakis, Papasotiriou, News Stand, Compendium, Ellinika Grammata
OR order directly from the ATHENS NEWS by sending an email to mangel@dolnet.gr

Gardening the traditional way

Landscape designer and Athens News columnist Jennifer Gay draws on a decade of experience in the Mediterranean to show you how to succeed in an environmentally friendly way. Whether you are coaxing climbers out of pots on a balcony or carving an oasis out of acres of scrubby hillside, this book offers invaluable advice on dealing with drought, pests, high winds, fires and soil erosion. Learn how to compost, mulch and turn one pest against another. Discover indigenous Greek species and the secrets of their survival. €17
On sale at Eleftheroudakis, Papasotiriou, News Stand, Compendium, Ellinika Grammata

Or order directly from the ATHENS NEWS by sending an email to mangel@dolnet.gr

Greece, a land of evergreen forests

Clearly laid out and stunningly illustrated, this book will take you far from the tourist-filled beaches and open your eyes to an area of Greece that deserves to be visited by everyone at least once. Discover Byzantine churches and Turkish mosques; silk towns, fur towns and even a reborn town; the legendary Mt Olympos and the mystical Meteora; the crystal-clear rivers of the Zagorohoria and the jagged peaks beyond.

Available at News Stand, Eleftheroudakis, Papasotiriou for €15.00
Or order NOW directly from the ATHENS NEWS by sending an email to mangel@dolnet.gr or phone 210-3333 735

every friday

Every Friday don't forget to pick up
the **ATHENS NEWS**

48 pages packed with in-depth reporting
and analysis of Greek life, including:

Greek and World News
Greek and World Business
Arts and Entertainment
Greek Escapes by Land and Sea
Foreign Communities
Greek Sport

Since 1952. **Greece in English.**

ATHENS NEWS

3 Christou Lada Street, 102 37 Athens, Greece
Tel (30-1) 3333.700 Fax (30-1) 3333.701
atheditor@dolnet.gr
www.athensnews.gr